Robert Graves

Robert Graves

A Biography

BRUCE KING

Haus Publishing

LONDON

First published in Great Britain in 2008 by Haus Publishing,
26 Cadogan Court, Draycott Avenue, London SW3 3BX
www.hauspublishing.co.uk

The moral rights of the author have been asserted

A CIP catalogue record for this book is available from the British Library

ISBN 978-1-905791-94-1

Typeset in Garamond by MacGuru Ltd
info@macguru.org.uk
Printed in Dubai by Oriental Press
Jacket illustration courtesy Getty Images

Contents

Introduction

It was a typical Deià party of the time, the summer of 1969. We put out bottles of wine, some beer, a few inexpensive snacks, left the door open, and went to the café until the party warmed up. Tomás and Juan Graves were DJing the music. When we returned it was wildish with everyone dancing, smoking and enjoying themselves. We were awakened the next morning by banging on the door. Robert Graves (1895–1985) demanded to know what happened to Juli Simon, his muse. Was she with us, was she at the party? He was afraid she was with the man she had left with; did we not know that she was pure and innocent and he might corrupt her with drugs?

Similar scenes occurred with other muses. Miranda Seymour and Martin Seymour-Smith tell of Graves taking a taxi from Deià to Soller where he burst into a cinema and accused the fiancé of Judith Bledsoe, his then intended muse, of not being good enough for her and corrupting her. The Spanish police put the man in jail for the night until the situation was straightened out.[1] Graves liked at times to fantasize that his woman was pure and innocent; he was perhaps closer to the truth when he complained of them as unfaithful and erratic. A typical Deià story told of a visiting English professor who wanted to see the latest muse, Cindy Lee, and was told that he could find her passed out under the table.

It was not just the muses, the supposed latest avatars of the White Goddess, who were unfaithful and devious, as even when Graves was still in a prolonged adolescent stage he idealized a schoolboy, 'Peter', thought him pure, and when others said that he was wrong, accepted Peter's claims of reform. Because a Canadian soldier reported that Peter tried to pick him up, in retaliation Graves would later risk his life by trying to humiliate and possibly cause the death of another Canadian officer.[2]

Female or male, the objects of his affection soon learned that Graves needed them much more than they needed him, that he needed to think of them as pure, and that he needed to be hurt to prove his devotion. Eventually either Graves or the other person would tire of the relationship, especially if it turned boringly domestic, and he would re-enact the drama with a new object of desire.

He knew he was being deceived and that in itself was part of the tension he required to be a writer. The objects of his desire were victims of his needs. His masochism was influenced by his relationship to his mother. Her distaste for sex and his own adolescent fear of the physical which found expression in homoeroticism may bring knowing smiles, especially as Graves hated his father. But the pattern Graves repeated is distinctive. Other virginal homosexuals have grown into straight old rams, but few, I imagine, had a desire to be submissive, play a conventional female role, and want to be emotionally and financially hurt by women as necessary to writing poetry while proclaiming that no one could imagine him homosexual.

Many artists produce art from wounds and pick away at the wound, but even by such standards Graves was an extreme case of contradictions. Thought a prude and aesthete, he became a boxer who threatened others. Although he avoided the Officer Training Corps at school and argued against going to war with Germany, he enlisted as soon as war was declared. His autobiography *Good-bye to All That* misleadingly says that he joined the services to avoid going to university and claims that he had already rejected the intense religiosity of his mother; actually he was a patriot who believed that God was on the side of England, and it was his duty to fight.

After surviving some of the major battles of the First World War, he was wounded by a German shell and wrongly thought to be and was declared dead. While the experience stayed with him throughout his life, it did not prevent his feeling that honour required him to return to the front line and he volunteered to be sent back. Suffering from shell shock, after the war he was unable to settle into a routine and was his own worst enemy. He stunned his homosexual friends and patrons by marrying a young feminist who thought that nothing any man suffered compared to the oppression of women.

Perhaps to show that she was right he fathered four

children on her in less than five years, and while he did all the housework, her health suffered and she resented him. Burdened with domestic work, trying to meet the fantasies of his wife, unable to find time to write to earn a living, he was often in poor health and did not finish his university degree.

Even more unusual was the invitation to Laura Riding to travel from America to accompany them to Egypt for an intended three years although Graves and his wife were financially broke, offered to pay her way, and only knew of her from a few poems and letters. Soon this threesome would become a tangled foursome and lead to Laura's attempted suicide, the separation of Graves from his wife who would take the four children and the other man, and the dominance of Laura over Graves as they created a private kingdom in a rural Majorcan village. It was here, for a time distant from the political rancour and horror of the 1930s, that Graves became a major writer under the humiliations and tutelage of his mistress who had become his master, while now denying him her bed, although apparently allowing him to bed others. For someone who disliked the avant-garde literature of his time he lived a very Modern life.

None of this gossip about his unconventionality would matter except that Graves was an excellent poet who wrote directly, and as a novelist indirectly, about his life. The classics of Modernism, the most powerful literary movement of the 20th century, expressed disillusionment with contemporary life through sceptical anti-epics. Whereas the major artists and theories of art during his time favoured impersonality, aesthetic distance and treated the personal with irony, he was a romantic who wrote about himself and his experience in some of the best short poems of the last century. He said he would outlast fashions because he was true to the muse of poetry.

Although most of his novels are based on his brilliant if eccentric scholarship, they either reflect the personal situations he was in at the time or are intended to prove his ideas. He claimed to have no imagination in the sense of a novelist or dramatist inventing plots, places and characters, but instead relied on his research to give him material for his prose fiction and eventually claimed to have rediscovered the ancient culture of the West, a retelling in which the heavens, earth, mythology and most of history and human behaviour were seen as part of a universal story that Graves had found and which he said was the source of his art and the life he lived.

The theme was his relationship to the Muse of Poetry, a goddess supposedly worshipped by the ancients, who fitfully made her presence in the woman the poet desired. In his daughter Lucia Graves' autobiography *A Woman Unknown* there is a presentation of his views and how firmly they became part of his character: 'For twenty years now he had maintained the unwavering belief that in preclassical times in Europe there existed a matriarchy presided over by an omnipotent goddess – the White Goddess – and he saw in the ecstatic worship of her followers the birth of poetic inspiration. Research led him to conclude that this matriarchal order had been supplanted by the Greek patriarchal system, which still persists to this day. The patriarchal social system was behind all our problems, my father would say, as he chopped vegetables or shelled peas in the kitchen. Male thinking – logical and scientific – took over from female thinking – changing the way the world was meant to be.'[3] While this myth of the White Goddess dominated his later decades the seeds can be seen in the fantasy of the pure young man waiting in England for Graves' return from the trenches in France. He needed to love and worship in order to create.

By the time of his death Graves was regarded as one of the most distinguished writers in English during the past century, a major poet, author of such best-selling novels as *I, Claudius* and *Claudius the God* and the famous autobiography *Good-bye to All That*, translator of many Greek and Roman classics, and someone who offered radically different versions of Greek, Jewish and Christian history along with, in *The White Goddess*, his own mythology. He was internationally honoured, translated into many languages, and his house in Majorca had become a national monument. His life – as a war poet, his mad love of Laura Riding, the home he created in Majorca, and his mythology of the White Goddess – made him a legend.

There are many facets of Graves that remain neglected, such as his detailed discussions of the sound of poetry, his criticism of empire, his place in the history of feminism, the ways he both rejected and shared characteristics of the Modernist movement in the arts, and his relationship to the counter-culture of the 1960s. In trying to understand what made him I risk adding to the legend, but with Graves the life and writing are entwined.

Unfortunately the self-assertion which allowed him to challenge convention also found expression in disagreeable behaviour towards others and at times a wilful blindness about himself. The sources of art, like Graves' objects of desire, are seldom pure.

Family and Charterhouse

1895–1914

When he was 34 years old Robert Graves wrote a now-famous autobiography, *Good-bye to All That*, which tells of his family, his childhood, early education, years in the army, marriage, studying at Oxford, months as a Professor in Egypt, and concludes with oblique allusions to a new woman in his life who will be his future in contrast to 'All That'. The autobiography uses Graves' early life to show the society and culture in which he was raised and which sent him and his generation to a senseless war in which the young were either killed or their lives so affected as to be wasted.

It is a brilliant book full of character sketches and the horrors of trench warfare, but it was dictated hurriedly in disturbed circumstances, and filled with mistakes and with malice towards those who disapproved of Graves' behaviour.

While for decades the autobiography was the basis of inter-pretations of Graves' life and work, *Good-bye to All That* is so often wrong in details that in places it is fiction. Aiming for a best-seller Graves had no hesitation about improving and inventing portions of the story; some parts are indeed fiction, from an unfinished novel he wrote earlier during the First World War. Twenty-eight years later when he revised *Good-bye to All That* for republication he further distorted the past.[4] As Graves seldom hesitated in revising history to justify himself, to see what he obscured and why, along with his foibles, obses-sions and the circumstances in which he wrote, helps towards understanding his writings.

Family

Robert von Ranke Graves was born on 24 July 1895, in the London suburb of Wimbledon. The family house was called Red Branch; the family was upper middle class, with some noble connections, on both sides. His father, Alfred Perceval Graves (1846–1931) was the second son of the Protestant Bishop of Limerick, and descended from a family with a long and notable history in Ireland and Scotland. While Graves often caricatured snobberies he was proud of being taken for and behaving like an aristocrat, superior to the bourgeois conventionality in which he was raised. He claimed his 'pedigree' went back to the Norman Conquest, and that the Graves came to Ireland with Cromwell. He wrote that the Scottish side 'was flawless right back to the medieval Scottish kings, to the two Balliols, the first and second Davids, and the Bruce'.[5] The family history of the Graves Family Association claims the family was originally called Da Grava and came from Bordeaux in Gascony, arrived with the Norman Conquest, and its many branches include such family names as Grave, Greve and Grieve. Alfred was of the 12th generation of Graves, his son Robert of the 13th.[6]

Charles (1812–99), the bishop, who signed himself Charles Limerick, was impressive, a classical scholar, an authority on the ancient Irish alphabet Ogham, a mathematician, and spoke many European languages. His wife Selina Cheyne, daughter of the Physician-General of the Forces in Ireland, had been a beauty. Charles and Selina knew many of the European cultural and scientific elite. Queen Victoria thought so highly of Charles' sermons that she gave him a ring with five diamonds.

The family included many poets and scholars including Alfred, Robert's father, a well-known poet and literary figure who wrote the then popular ballad 'Father O'Flynn', and whose publishing and reviewing connections were useful to his son. Alfred, however, lacked the financial touch. He sold the rights to 'Father O'Flynn' for little, although after Alfred's death Robert would still earn royalties from the song.[7] Alfred taught his son verse forms and Irish ballads; he was also an authority on Welsh songs which he translated into English and was made a Welsh bard.

Robert when young was also taught how to make Bardic rhymes.[8] His unusual sensitivity towards patterns of sounds, assonance and kinds of rhyming, along with his early poems in folk and ballad form were influenced by his father. His later treatment in *The White Goddess* of such obscurities as the language of trees and the supposed significance of ancient Irish alphabets continued a family tradition, a tradition he knew from his father and his father's books, some inherited from his grandfather, which later became part of his own library.

Alfred was a school inspector by profession, a well-known reformer whose accomplishments included making sports compulsory. Far from wealthy, he was careful with money and wanted his children to earn their education through being awarded scholarships: he favoured careers likely to provide a secure, stable income. Robert claimed to hate him because of his financial caution and refusal to accept that his children wanted different lives than those he planned for them. The latter was more significant as Robert often appealed to him when financially desperate and his father interceded on his behalf with his mother who had inherited money which she invested wisely. Father and son at times discussed co-operating on literary works.

Part of his dislike of his father resulted from competition; Alfred was a success in the literary world and earning from his writings during decades when his son was unsuccessfully trying to live by his pen and near destitution. In *Good-bye to All That* Robert's seeming praise of his father rapidly becomes ironic and then sarcastic. 'Some of his songs I sing without prejudice; when washing up after meals or shelling peas or on similar occasions. He never once tried to teach me how to write, or showed any understanding of my serious work; he was always more ready to ask advice about his own work than to offer it for mine.' He claimed he learned writing from his mother rather than his father.[9] He learned from both. The bitterness noticeable in his later comments on male rivals for the affections of women would be especially nasty.

Alfred's wife, Amaliae (Amy) von Ranke Graves (1857–1951), was of German birth. A model of Victorian ethical behaviour and prudery, Amaliae had come to England to be a lady's companion; when after the woman's death she learned that she had been made her heir, she insisted the fortune be divided among the disinherited family. In 1891 she married Alfred who already had five children, Philip, Molly, Richard, Perceval and Susan, by a wife who died of tuberculosis in 1886; he needed a mother for his children and that role appealed to Amy, who was seeking a vocation. Taking care of Alfred's children was more appealing than going to India as a missionary. It was partly an arranged marriage planned by the family, although Alfred needed to woo her. Their marriage renewed a not-distant family tie between Helena Clarissa Graves (1808–71) and the historian Leopold von Ranke (1795–1886). It was Lily who thought of bringing the widowed Alfred and her older sister Amy together.[10]

Alfred respected Amy but did not love her; the children held them together. Although Amy had a further five children with Alfred she had an ideal of women as pure saintly creatures; she claimed that sexual intercourse was disgusting and only to be used for procreation. She and Alfred had two daughters, then Robert, then two more sons, Charles and John. From an early age the children were introduced to writing poetry as part of their life. Amy made up songs and rhymes, sang hymns, told stories and created a magazine for her children for their rhymes and poems. Soon they were writing their own small poems.[11] Clarissa (1892–1976), Rosaleen (1894–1989) and Robert were to become poets, Charles (1899–1971) became a journalist, and John (1903–80) a headmaster who planned to write a biography of Robert, a task continued by his son Richard Perceval Graves. Eventually Rosaleen became a doctor and a musician. Her papers on musicology can be found in specialized journals.

There were other ways in which Robert continued the culture of his family. He thought of himself as Irish, an Irish Protestant; he justified his elaborations on truth as Irish romanticism and storytelling, and he paraded his knowledge of Celtic literature while carrying on the tradition of classic and Celtic scholarship. He knew German, French, Spanish, Latin and Greek; he, like Amy, invested in property, and assumed that servants were a normal part of life. He had a large family and he was distant from his children. He played sports. Like his father he worked incessantly to support his family. Even his hatreds, such as schoolteaching, prudence and financial caution, were a reaction to his father.

His grandfather Charles, the Bishop of Limerick, was one of six children. Robert amusingly wrote that the Bishop had 'eight or was it ten', but the actual number was nine. Alfred's children totalled ten.[12] Graves would have eight. Such parents were distant. His father was seldom home as he was busy with his work and literary career, while his mother had a full social and charitable life. The children were raised by servants who were expected to address them by the honorific 'Master' or 'Miss' and by a nurse who occupied a middle place in the hierarchy between servants and family. With such a large family to care for, the servants were overworked and few stayed long. Robert and the other children learned class and religious prejudice from their surroundings as those who waited on them were far less privileged or educated; the servants' rooms were badly furnished, without carpeting or wardrobes.[13] Except for the presence of the nurse, who effectively replaced their mother, the children had to depend upon themselves for companionship.

Robert claimed that in such a large family the children became indistinguishable to their parents and that he was often called by the name of others. That he was raised in such a family, and that he should mention the distance of his parents and the lack of companionship beyond other children and their nurse, might account for his intense need for love and why in the future he often had friends living with him who were expected to be involved in each other's work. He seemed lonely and unable to be at ease in the setting of a small nuclear family or on his own; the unhappiness of his first marriage would lead to others being invited in.

The lives of the two sets of his father's children often intersected. Robert got along with his sisters and half-brothers but intensely disliked his younger brothers. Richard had a career in the consular service and Robert would cross his path in Cairo; Richard would much later invite his now famous half-brother to Israel. Philip worked in Intelligence. Because so many in various branches of the family for generations had similar names it is easy to become confused by who is a brother, half-brother, uncle, nephew or some other relation. Besides grandfather Charles, there was an uncle Charles who was a journalist for *The Spectator* and useful to Robert in the literary world. Robert's younger brother Charles was also a successful journalist and Robert hated him. John, following in his father's footsteps, became a schoolteacher which Robert thought offensive in its normality; whenever a teacher appears in his writings he is usually a caricature of John.

Amy dressed in an old-fashioned, proper, dowdy fashion, and although she had inherited wealth she was more than prudent with money. She was, however, willing to invest in property. Some of the best times of Robert's youth were summer holidays among her German relatives or at a house she had built in Wales.[14]

The happiest writing in *Good-bye to All That* is of visits with German relatives. Robert liked the food, the strange places, the different customs. There was an interesting variety of aunts and uncles including an uncle who owned a peacock farm and an Aunt Agnes married to a Baron Siegfried who lived in a 9th-century castle in the Bavarian Alps. Aufsess Castle was filled with armour and other treasures such as a mysterious 12th-century chest which could only be opened with two keys and no one knew what was in it. A grandfather had restored a former shooting lodge of the kings of Bavaria which had a magnificent banqueting hall with stained glass windows which to Robert as a child 'seemed as big as a cathedral'.[15] On the estate there was a carp pond and the servants stood at attention when his grandfather drove past.

Germany was emotionally important to Robert. It represented the happiness of youth before the tensions and conflicts of puberty. Knowing that many of his relatives were Germans would leave him with deep feelings of guilt for the German soldiers he killed during the First World War because they might have been his relatives. It is likely that his views concerning an original matriarchy were influenced by a 19th-century Swiss German cultural anthropologist. He spoke German well and in old age when he suffered from Alzheimer's Disease and regressed to memories of his youth, he sometimes spoke German rather than English.

The Welsh connection was also important to him although it was recent and started when his mother during 1897 bought land and the next year built a house, Erinfa, on the north coast at Harlech, followed by other land and houses nearby. A village 500 feet up on a range of hills with a castle, Harlech had a plain and beach and to the north was wild country. Behind the village there were desolate rocky hills which appealed to Graves for its sense of independence.[16] The seasons appeared to remain unchanging; the hills were cold, had strong winds, few trees or birds except the odd buzzard. Beyond a few sheep there was little company. During school holidays Robert enjoyed Harlech where he and his sister Rosaleen collected folk songs. To recover his sanity he would return there and walk the hills when on leave from the army and he imagined retiring there after the war. Later when he left England for Deià, Majorca, it was like returning to the mountainous Wales of his youth.

Moral terror

The children were brought up in an environment of extreme discipline in which turning down the page of a book or leaving a book face down was cause for punishment. This may have contributed to John's nervous breakdown. Miranda Seymour observes that three of the children had nervous breakdowns before they were thirty.[17] Amy preached high moral standards throughout her life and would write to her son at school reminding him of his duties and failures. He lived in terror of his mother's expectations. His life as an adult often replays his relationship with his mother. How could you please such a woman? How could you be certain of her love? His later strange worship of Laura Riding seems a replacement for his mother's discipline.

At the age of seven he signed a pledge, which his mother saved, to be a teetotaler, and it was not until the Sixth Form at school that he drank anything alcoholic. Few would be able to keep to her expected standards of saintliness and demands for self-sacrifice. In his novel *Count Belisarius* the narrator objects to Belisarius' mother making him swear an oath 'renouncing the world, the flesh, and the devil' before he was old enough to understand; the result could only be feelings of guilt later in life. At school and even in the army Robert was embarrassed by bawdy humour and language.[18]

His childhood had a lasting effect on him in that he rejected and rebelled against his parents' discipline, guilt-making and prudery, yet what he was rebelling against had formed him and was part of himself. His religious beliefs lasted into the war years and his experience as a soldier. Although in *Good-bye to All That* he states that the war ended his religiosity this is not correct. As his biographers have demonstrated, he remained attracted to Christianity as late as 1918 and fears of damnation and sin continued in his poetry into the early 1920s.[19] His later studies of the life of Jesus and the Hebrew Myths and his discovery of a supposed pre-historic mythology of goddess worship can be seen as an attempt to replace the Christianity of the first decades of his life.

The demand for purity would especially affect Graves' feelings towards sexuality. 'My religious training developed in me a great capacity for fear (I was perpetually tortured by the fear of hell), a superstitious conscience and a sexual embarrassment. I was very long indeed in getting rid of all this.' The passages concerning nudity in *Good-bye to All That* are closely associated with sexual fears as when a description of his horror of bathing nude is followed by passages of terror at women and sexuality: 'there was an open-air swimming bath where all the boys bathed naked, and I was overcome by horror at the sight. There was one boy there of nineteen with red hair, real bad, Irish, red hair all over his body. I had not know that hair grew on bodies'. This is immediately followed by: 'And the headmaster had a little daughter with a little girl friend, and I was in a sweat of terror whenever I met them; because, having no brothers, they once tried to find out about male anatomy from me.' Next he remembers feeling whispered about while awaiting his sisters at their school which resulted in nightmares years later, and he recalls when he was seventeen a girl tried to make love to him and his being 'so frightened I could have killed her'. Graves accuses the British public school system for forming homosexuals and what he calls 'pseudo-homosexuals', by which he means men who are romantically attracted towards other men but remain 'chaste and sentimental'.[20] Throughout his youth and into his twenties he thought sexual intercourse, in contrast to affection, was disgusting.

Later in life he would hate his normal feelings of lust and this contributed to his unconsummated attraction towards men, his long virginity and his strange domination by the women he did bed, as if he could only justify sex through idealizing women as goddesses whom he served. The fullest expression of this conflict would occur in the creation of the myth of the White Goddess, a demanding muse of poetry who would for a time descend on some woman to whom he was attracted. Desire was transformed through the drama of courtship into poetry.

Charterhouse

His early education seems unlikely for the son of a school inspector and educational reformer. First in 1902 there was an exceptionally bad school in Wimbledon where he was expected to learn the 23-times table. Or so he claimed. About six months later, now seven, he was sent to King's College, Wimbledon, where, the youngest pupil, he learned dirty words before Alfred removed him for three years to Rokeby, a local preparatory school, until, aged 11, he was sent away to a prep school in Rugby with the expectation he would earn a scholarship to a public school. He was unhappy there, failed a scholarship exam to Winchester, and returned to Rugby for a short time before a scandal caused the headmaster to flee. Robert next went to Copthorne, a preparatory school in Sussex with high standards and a respect for learning, where he was happy for a year. Alfred, however, feared that Robert would not win a scholarship to Winchester as Greek was his weakest subject and instead sent him to Charterhouse where he earned first place and some years of misery.[21]

Graves gained a Charterhouse scholarship and became a boarder when he was fourteen. Charterhouse was at this time an inappropriate place for a serious, prudish young scholar; he claimed it was dominated by those who enjoyed homosexuality and by wealthy students who had few cultural interests. Graves was thought priggish and quickly became unpopular especially as he was said to be of German Jewish origin. In his defence he claimed to be Irish, which turned another boy at school, who was Irish, against him; throughout most of his life Graves would see himself as a romantic Irishman rather than a phlegmatic, practical Englishman. Brought up in a family which honoured culture, examination results and noble work, he was soon unhappy at Charterhouse and an obvious victim for bullies especially as rather than ignoring them he argued back. His interest in poetry was thought suspect, he claimed to have no interest in sports and lacked the money to treat others. He begged his parents to let him return home and when they did not he hated them. He did, however, at the suggestion of a fellow pupil, Raymond Rodakowski, learn to box as a means of self-defence and this eventually improved his standing at school and later in the army. Raymond became a close friend, a friendship which did not last beyond Robert's discovering that his friend no longer believed in Christianity. 'I put religion and my chances of salvation before human love.' [22]

He had more than a streak of being a bully himself. Early in *Good-bye to All That* he brags of his ability to act superior to get what he wants; later his haughtiness would offend the poet Edmund Blunden and others. He acted and would spend like an aristocrat. His feelings of superiority were often expressed in his behaviour towards others. He admits at the age of twelve despising the nurse at home as she was less educated than himself and a Baptist, and 'that if I struggled with her I was able to trip her up and bruise her quite easily'. Miranda Seymour says that he was 'a quarrelsome bully' at Rokeby. He began bullying his younger brother Charles at an early age and he could be brutal. Richard Perceval Graves writes that Charles, after being thrown to the ground and having his arm twisted, threatened to revenge himself when older and stronger by killing Robert. Even John was often hurt by Robert's blows. [23]

Visiting him at Charterhouse, his sister Rosaleen found

Robert 'difficult', 'self important' and looking for fights. He was far from passive when tormented by bullies at Charterhouse where he even threatened his teachers; he was a powerful boxer and was thought socially aggressive and opinionated by other officers in the army. Graves was seldom docile or compliant; he was stubborn, defiant, rebellious and likely to harm others who annoyed him. He seemed to be seeking fights, and as quick with his fists as with insulting words.[24] His going his own way in his marriages, affairs with women, rebellion against the values of his parents, claim to say 'Good-bye to All That' and his creation of a strange mythology and religion, developed from his assertion of himself physically, verbally and spiritually. If he had a corresponding need later in life to be dominated by woman he was at least as much the pursuer and in charge of his humiliation as they.

Sexuality

There is a parallel between Graves' view of boxing and his attitude towards sex and sexual relationships according to which the giving and taking of pain is part of the pleasure. He even writes of boxing as sacramental. 'There is a lot of sexual feeling in boxing – the dual play, the reciprocity, the pain not felt as pain. The exhibition match to me had something of the quality that Dr. Marie Stopes would call sacramental.'[25] The invocation of Stopes, the famous feminist advocate of family planning and contraception as well as equality between the sexes, and her notion of lovemaking as itself sacred or sacramental, indicates how boxing, with its mutual masochism, was connected in his feelings with sexual love. Bonding and sexual pleasure required pain.

Boxing was part of his friendship with Raymond; after breaking with him, he returned to playing rugby. Indeed for all Graves' complaints about the importance of sports at Charterhouse and his assertions that he was not interested in them, he was more of an athlete than one might expect; he was a boxer, played rugby – at which he broke his nose – skied, learned to climb, and later played hockey.[26] As with much else he says about himself at Charterhouse his comments about sports in *Good-bye to All That* seem distorted for a purpose. He was highly competitive whether at sports, playing cards, or in such social entertainments as singing and telling anecdotes. Between servants, attending a famous public school and having aristocratic family relations, Robert easily took on the airs of the well-born, acted superior, and liked to win.

He always knew he wanted to be a poet, which he thought of as an occupation. Except for a short period teaching in Cairo he would have no other occupation than as a writer. Although he claimed to have fallen in love with poetry while at Charterhouse, he, as the son of Alfred and Amy, had always been involved with writing. By the time he was three he had made rhyming couplets. When his brother John was born on 24 February 1903, Robert wrote a celebratory quatrain.[27] By the time he was twelve he was writing what Alfred considered real poems. Soon he learned 'to write a Welsh *englyn* according to the fixed ninety-odd rules' which was published in his father's

Welsh Poetry Old and New (1913). In 1912 Robert and his sisters Clarissa and Rosaleen wrote light and nonsense verses which his father sent to *Punch* and then more successfully to *The Children's Encyclopedia* and *The Children's Newspaper*. By the time he was fifteen at Charterhouse he published a poem, 'The Mountain Side at Evening', in *The Carthusian*, the school magazine.[28] Because of this he was invited to join the short-lived Poetry Society, contributed poems and other writings to school periodicals, and became friends with those who also devoted themselves to literature. The Poetry Society was dissolved by the authorities after it was found that a poem was about homosexual love between two students. It is probably an indication of his future caution that Graves was the one who identified the author and those involved.[29]

While at school he formed intense emotional attachments and became increasingly conscious of his emotions, distinguishing those who were so inclined from others, but he remained terrified of physical intercourse and claimed to drop the friendships of those who were sexually active. Much of *Good-bye to All That* is concerned with homosexual love. 'Poetry and Dick were now the only two things that really mattered.' [30] 'Dick' was the name he gave in *Good-bye to All That* to George Harcourt Johnstone (1899–1949), more usually referred to as 'Peter', a younger boy at Charterhouse towards whom Robert was emotionally attracted for almost a decade. Peter was an aristocrat from Yorkshire, in the school choir and had a taste for such poets of the French decadence as Baudelaire and Verlaine whom he discussed with Graves. The

crush started in 1913, led to other students mocking Robert
– which resulted in fights for which he was nearly expelled
when a fellow monitor scratched RG and GJ on a wall above
twinned hearts.[31] He wrote to Peter while in the army and
when their paths crossed at Oxford, after Graves had married,
the meeting was emotionally charged.

He could be naive and hasty. When he learned of a teacher's
supposed involvement with Peter he confronted the teacher
and demanded his resignation.[32] Whenever he was told of
Peter's sexual activity he believed Peter's claim to limit himself
to Platonic love or accepted his explanations that he was just
fooling about.

Graves' references to homosexuality seem charged with
conflict. Why accuse Charterhouse of being a hotbed of
homosexuality when he was himself attracted, although not
practising? And why blame Charterhouse when he would
write in *Good-bye to All That* that homosexual feelings were
a common experience at British public schools? He also did
not mention that he had continued such friendships later.
In the revised 1957 edition of *Good-bye to All That* he would
further tone down his schoolboy homoeroticism and declare
his dislike of homosexuals.

Mallory and Marsh

Graves' schoolboy poetry was old-fashioned and much like his
father's; it began to change after he met George Mallory and
Edward Marsh. While at Charterhouse Graves became friends

with a new teacher, George Mallory (1886–1924), who told him about such contemporaries as George Bernard Shaw, H G Wells, John Masefield and Rupert Brooke. Mallory recommended to Graves the writings of Samuel Butler (1835–1902) author of the anti-Utopian satire *Erewhon* (1872) – an influence on Graves' later *Seven Days in New Crete* (1949, American title *Watch the North Wind Rise*) – and Butler's posthumously published autobiographical novel *The Way of All Flesh* (1903) with its intense criticism of Victorian morality and the ways family, schools and institutions inhibit and deform the self. This reinforced Robert's own long-felt anger at what he felt were attempts by others to dominate him. Mallory was an internationally famous mountaineer who would die on his third attempt to scale Mount Everest. Graves learned from Mallory how to climb, a skill he never lost. I would watch with admiration as even in his seventies he would use only his fingers to climb or descend the steep cliff overhanging the small rocky cove at Deià although his mind was already going.

Mallory was his entry to part of the London literary establishment. Mallory knew the poet Rupert Brooke who introduced them to Edward Marsh, founder of the Georgian poets and editor of Georgian anthologies which were meant originally as a rebellion against the ornate language and high sentiments of Victorian poetry. Graves would call Marsh 'the Father of modern English Poetry'.[33]

Edward Marsh (1872–1953) had been one of the famous and usually homosexual Apostles at Cambridge University. Through his connection with the influential man of letters

Edmund Gosse he met Robert Ross, one of Oscar Wilde's circle, who introduced him to the London cultural world. Marsh seemed to know everyone worth knowing. Besides being a patron of the arts and a collector of paintings and with Rupert Brooke the founder of the Georgians, he was a civil servant often assigned as a private secretary to powerful government ministers. Winston Churchill trusted him and Marsh followed him through his various ministries. Later in 1939 Marsh would write *A Number of People* (1939) about the artists and politicians he had known.

Between 1911 and 1922 there were five *Georgian Poetry* anthologies that included such writers as Rupert Brooke, Edmund Blunden, D H Lawrence, Isaac Rosenberg, Walter de la Mare, Siegfried Sassoon, Robert Nichols and Graves. Their meeting place was Harold Monro's Poetry Bookshop where in 1914 Graves first met the then little-known Robert Frost. Although Frost was two decades older than Graves they respected and got along with each other. Graves would praise Frost, along with Thomas Hardy, in his Hogarth Press publication *Contemporary Techniques of Poetry: A Political Analogy* (1925). He would not see Frost again until 1957 when they met up in London, and then in 1959 and 1960 by which time they were both famous.[34]

Although their rebellion would soon appear old-fashioned as their work was overtaken by the radical imagist and cubist aesthetics of the international Modernist movement and such writers as Pound, Joyce and Eliot, originally the Georgians were a step in that direction. Their writing was less mannered than had been common and they were in favour of plain, natural language, realistic observation and direct expression of feelings. This might be described as the first phase of Georgian poetry. Unfortunately there was a second phase when John C Squire (1884–1958) edited the Georgian anthologies, and the movement became known for quaint, popular, mannered verse about rural delights. Squire also founded and edited *London Mercury*, which became a citadel of anti-modernism; it was known as his 'squirearchy'.

Marsh was helpful in getting Graves published and in bringing him to the notice of others in the literary world. That Graves was intense, full lipped, with grey eyes, and a large head of unruly black curly hair, strongly built, six foot two inches tall, physically attractive and that Marsh was homosexual meant that many of those Graves met, such as Siegfried Sassoon, were also homosexual and such were the friendships he would form and which would form his view of himself. Many of those whom Graves met in the arts, such as the highly successful songwriter Ivor Novello, were introduced by or through Marsh. Over the decades Marsh would be useful, lending Graves money, helping with the police after Laura Riding's attempted suicide, and pushing Graves' novel *I, Claudius* for a Hawthornden award. Having been introduced to the literary world through an homosexual network it is not surprising that it took two decades before Graves untangled himself from it, despite his later protests that he was a heterosexual who hated homosexuals.

3

Soldier Poet and Sex

1914–18

Graves had been awarded a Classics scholarship at St John's, Oxford, but when Germany invaded Belgium on 4 August 1914, bringing Britain into the war on the side of France and Russia, he volunteered and was immediately accepted for military service as a commissioned officer in the Royal Welch Fusiliers, a famous regiment which traced its history to 1690 and the Battle of the Boyne. Being from a public school and having family connections helped; an uncle-in-law was Admiral Sir Richard Poore.[35] His parents were proud of him, for a change, and he was proud of the regiment, loyal to it, and in old age would note the anniversaries of its battles, write to others who served in the regiment, and gave the impression that it was the one society to which he had and still belonged.

Serving in the army appealed to his sense of honour – it was the duty of a gentleman – and he began with enthusiasm. Soon reality conflicted with his idealism and puritanism. After a few weeks training he was sent in September 1914 to an internment camp for aliens where the fifty soldiers under him when not guarding prisoners were chasing local women. 'Oh, and Oh!', a poem he wrote at the time, contrasts such, to him, sordid lust

Loutish he
And sluttish she
In loathsome love together press

with his love of 'Peter' Johnstone: 'Far away lives my darling'.[36] The camp also contrasted his notions of honour and duty with the ways of the world. His soldiers kept deserting to chase women; his desire to be sent to the Front was frustrated because he was told he did not dress well enough for an officer and he had to purchase a new wardrobe. Such ironies would keep occurring; army life even during the Great War mirrored the social conventions and snobberies of England.

Before being sent to France he had several leaves during which he visited Charterhouse where he became sentimental, saw Peter again, and in London visited with Edward Marsh who told him to avoid such fusty diction as 'thee' and 'thou', and was displayed by his proud parents. His brothers were too young to enlist and his half-brothers were employed in positions that the government thought necessary. Although British relatives were already at the front so was the German side of the family. As many of the British and German upper classes were related the war pitted various branches of families against each other. Amy had news during the war of the deaths and honours on the German side of the family. Visiting London, Robert found that Red Branch House was let and his parents were staying in a house owned by his uncle Robert von Ranke, the former German Consul in London who, leaving England hurriedly, put his home in Amy's care.[37] Later, visiting Harlech, Robert found that Erinfa was occupied by Belgian refugees who told stories of German atrocities. He was promoted to lieutenant although his only fighting was a boxing match, followed by a week sparring with a sergeant who would win the welterweight championship.

After ten months in England he was sent, in mid-May 1915, to command a platoon of forty soldiers near the Front in France. By now the front line consisted of many thousands of miles of trenches usually reinforced by a second line of reserve trenches and further back more trenches for supplies; with each side dug into heavily defended positions there would be no major change in positions from late November 1914 until the Allied offensives beginning in July 1918. The war was impersonal and the soldiers were victims of a new form of mass warfare with such new weapons as poison gas about which they could do little, but there was also the need to be heroic, to assert oneself, to be honourable, to get revenge.

At first Graves was in solidly-built former French trenches ten to fifteen yards from the Germans and he was bravely nonchalant about the exchanges of gunfire, the machine guns, bombing, and the dead. He even posted souvenirs home.

By now the army was taking anyone it could get; his platoon ranged from a 15- to a 63-year-old. There was the continual sound of gunfire and bombardments; on his first watch he discovered the dead body of a soldier who committed suicide. It was impossible to stay at the front for longer than three days without risking a breakdown. Although Graves had collapses he wrote letters home in a deceptively light-hearted tone, some of which his uncle Charles published in *The Spectator*.

He was an excellent soldier with a strong sense of duty and loyalty to the men he commanded, although once more he was felt to be an outsider who could not bond with the others. Their rough language and sexual talk embarrassed him. To the other officers he appeared to be a know-it-all with opinions on everything, which he was too willing to share. Siegfried Sassoon said that Graves was always giving opinions without being asked.[38] This remained a fault throughout his life; he insensitively expected others to share his interests and listen to his views. He always dressed badly, but in an army officer such sloppiness was inappropriate.

In France Graves was once more complaining about the sexual conduct of others. In Le Havre he claimed that little boys pimped for their sisters. Just behind the front a local farmer's daughter tried to tempt him by lifting her skirt to show a thigh wound. Disgusted by his soldiers going to brothels, he was unwilling to admit to his prudery and pretended he feared becoming diseased. While avoiding the local brothel he continued writing to his schoolfriend Peter who was often on his mind and was the muse of several poems of this period, especially '1915' in *Over the Brazier* (1916). Graves was upset by a letter from a cousin telling him that Peter Johnstone was not an innocent. Soon Johnstone wrote admitting guilt but saying that he would change his behaviour because of his friendship with Robert. During August Graves wrote to Peter that if he died he wanted to be remembered and would leave him all his books and friends.[39] The love poem, '1915', contrasts life in the trenches with England; in it Peter is the equivalent of the lover, symbolic of peace, whom the soldier misses and to whom he hopes to return.

> Dear, you've been everything that I most lack
> In these soul-deadening trenches – pictures, books
> Music, the quiet of an English wood,
> Beautiful comrade-looks ...[40]

Peter is associated with the arts along with the homoerotic ('Beautiful comrade-looks'). It is a foretaste of Graves' later relationships to the women in his life that Johnstone easily deceived a prudish soldier who wanted pure love.

The Front

Graves continued to write poetry at the Front, describing the fighting, dead bodies and other horrors he saw. His war poetry stuck to clear language to describe what he saw; often it made comparisons to memories of childhood or took the perspective of a child. Unlike the other war poets he did not write patriotic rhetoric, seldom wrote nostalgically of peacetime England, or later write protests against war. Marsh had advised him to keep his poetry simple, clear and direct and that is what he did, or tried to do. While there is a silent contrast between the sonnet form of 'Limbo' and its language and subject matter the poem suffers somewhat from the obviousness of the rhymes:

Can't sleep, must lie awake with the horrid sound
That roars and whirs and rattles overhead
All day, all night, and jars and tears the ground[41]

He would write his poems on any paper he had available, including letters and envelopes. He also read whenever he could.

In June he and his men were in Vermeilles which had been taken and retaken eight times since the previous October; the original excitement of being at the front was over and danger had subsided into repetition. By August 1915 Graves was making night patrols across no-man's-land into German territory where to survive he sometimes had to huddle among dead soldiers until he could get word back of the German position for bombardments. A poem, 'I Hate the Moon', contrasts the usual poetic associations of the moon with the danger of night patrols under full moonlight. Like most of his poetry it was based on an actual experience and was written after patrolling near Cuichy where the Germans and British lines were so close that they shared the 20–30-foot high brick-stacks from which they shot into each other's trenches. During September he was on leave in England then returned to France where there was a major offensive, the Battle of Loos, which began with some initial success on 25 September, but after three days the army had lost over 20,000 men and was in retreat. This was the first time the British had used gas in the war. Fighting continued until mid-October.

He was at the front with the Royal Welch who, on 25 September, were sent on suicidal attacks as decoys for the main offensive at Loos to the south. The whole operation was a disaster. The authorities decided that the soldiers should go into battle without their winter kit which they had to return to barracks at Béthune. Then they had to march once more, back to Cambrin, although they lacked sleep, were cold, and the main road was choked with soldiers and transport vehicles. There seemed no logical connection between what was being asked of the soldiers and how it might affect their conduct in the coming likely suicidal battle. Once it started everything that could go wrong, did go wrong.

The British attack began with poison gas but the wind was blowing in the wrong direction. As the men panicked the German began intense shelling and the British artillery bombarded their own troops. Two companies of the Royal Welch Fusiliers were destroyed and while Graves waited to continue the attack an adjunct decided that this was suicide and sent for further orders. After hours among shells, gas and the dead, Graves was told that the attack was called off. He was the only survivor of the group of five officers who had arrived with him.

Another attack on 27 September began with poison gas but this time it was soon called off. He had little sleep for over a week and to avoid breaking down he was drinking a bottle of whisky a day. The Battle of Loos continued. By now it was obvious that a generation was being sacrificed by incompetent commanders in a war that seemed unlikely to end. Graves, who remained religious, accepted the situation as God-given. 'The Face of the Heavens', a poem written at this time, concludes

You may tell God's mood:
He shines, rains, thunders,
But all his works are good.[42]

In October the Royal Welch were allowed to leave the Front. Graves was disillusioned, felt close to breaking and wrote to his father asking him to use influence to get him transferred to England. Instead he was ordered to return to the trenches where after six days he was made a captain and sent, in November, to be billeted with the First Battalion which was trying to dig new trenches in the frozen marsh. When they were sent back from the front to Picardy for further training Graves cheered up. He came across Siegfried Sassoon who at twenty-nine was almost ten years older, and immediately liked him, although he thought his poetry sentimental and rhetorical about the war. They shared an interest in literature, knew some of the same people, and were to become close friends.

Sassoon

Siegfried Sassoon (1886–1967) was the son of a rich Persian Jew who married into a British Anglican family; his older brother Hamo was a well-known sculptor. Siegfried – his first name derived from his mother's love of Wagnerian opera – was a cricketer, huntsman and self-published poet who began writing verse with high-flying sentiments that would later change to anti-war protest. He joined the army but before being sent to France broke his arm when riding. Before he had recovered he joined the Royal Welch Fusiliers as an officer, serving from May 1915 until April 1917. He was sent to France in November 1915. After the deaths of his brother Hamo at Gallipoli in 1915 and a friend, David Thomas, he became obsessed with taking revenge on the Germans and was extremely brave. His exploits earned him the nickname 'Mad Jack'.

Aware of his homosexuality, he cultivated similar friends whom he introduced to Graves. And until Graves decided to change his sexual orientation it was assumed by Sassoon and others that Graves was homosexual, an assumption he himself shared. This is a different Robert Graves to that portrayed in *Good-bye to All That* where he has a schoolboy crush on 'Dick', a past which he will later try to erase. About the attraction of Sassoon and Graves towards other men there is no doubt as they exchanged letters on the subject.

Martin Seymour-Smith makes a distinction between pederasts and the non-practising homosexuals influenced by the Aesthetic Movement of the 1890s, but Seymour-Smith also assumes that it was to prove himself heterosexual that Graves soon married a woman whom Seymour-Smith claims he did not love.[43] As Seymour-Smith was a close friend and his biography is more defence than analytical this was probably Graves' own view of his past. By now Graves' circle of friends were homosexual and as openly so as the period allowed when homosexuality was still a serious crime. Besides Marsh and Sassoon and Peter Johnstone there was the effete George Devenish and Robert Ross – a lover and literary executor of Oscar Wilde – whom Graves met through Sassoon during 1916.

As Ross, until his death in 1918, remained a friend of Graves, it is useful to remember that 'Robbie' was not only openly gay but was nationally known for being so. Even before Wilde's trial there was a scandal when Ross and Lord Alfred Douglas had sex with 14- and 15-year-old boys at Ross' house. It had required much persuasion to prevent the parents going to the police. Later Lord Alfred, who wanted to live down his past, kept trying to have Ross arrested for homosexuality. Graves had joined what was, during the war, a well-known circle of homosexuals whom Ross had gathered around himself, including Sassoon and later Wilfred Owen.

That Graves identified himself with those who were 'so' is clear from a letter he wrote on 2 May 1916 to Sassoon about the poet Charles Sorley who was killed by sniper fire on 13 October 1915 during the Battle of Loos. Sorley, like Sassoon, was educated at Marlborough College and his *Marlborough and Other Poems* (1916) had recently been published. Graves asks 'was he "so"?'. As evidence of the likelihood that Sorley was homosexual Graves says 'As his book contains no conventional love-lyrics and as he'd reached the age of 20, I conclude he was.'[44] Miranda Seymour points out that the only love poem Graves had written then was to Peter. Although throughout his life Graves denied ever having been homosexual, his letters to Sassoon make clear that then he thought he was. On 27 May 1916, he wrote to Sassoon mocking Peter Johnstone's mother who had found and been shocked by letters from Graves with their 'modern ideas' and forbid her son to have any further contact until leaving Charterhouse. Graves mocked this 'disaster: I am widowed, laid waste and desolate'. In his letter Peter told Robert he would never forget him and after a few years they could resume their relationship. Graves hoped Peter would soon rebel against his mother, but Graves also wrote to Sassoon about a new 18-year-old boyfriend which helped take his mind off Peter.[45]

First death

The great Battle of the Somme started in July 1916; before it was over approximately a quarter of a million soldiers would die. It was one of the most futile battles of an increasingly futile war as soldiers advanced into German machine-gun fire; before it finished heavy rain had turned the trenches and front into pure mud which swallowed the soldiers and their equipment whether they were attacking or in defensive positions. The British hoped that this would be a breakthrough but it ended in another failure. During July Graves and Sassoon met, and discussed living and travelling together if they survived the war. Graves wrote and sent Sassoon his famous poem about the dead Boche. The Royal Welch Fusiliers were in reserve just behind the front lines waiting to replace the dying when on 20 July 1916, just before he turned 21, Graves was hit by fragments from a German shell that exploded behind him. He remained partly conscious for a while but lost consciousness and was expected to die. Two days later an official letter was sent notifying his parents of his death and a report was carried by *The Times*, which later offered to publish a retraction for free.

After being thought dead he was found to be breathing, regained consciousness, relapsed into unconsciousness again, slowly regained consciousness and while in great pain was sent to a field hospital and then to a hospital in Rouen. After ten days he returned to England to recover. The wounds were not bad, but his right lung was damaged and for a time he had trouble standing. He suffered throughout his life from shell shock. Sassoon, not knowing he had survived, wrote 'To His Dead Body'. Graves tried making a joke of his reported death and even bragged to Marsh that he wanted to convince Peter to reproach his mother for having prohibited any contact with the poor dead soldier.[46]

Sassoon had also been sent back to England with lung problems from his time in the trenches. He and Graves tried recuperating at Erinfa, the house in Harlech, Wales, which Amy had built during 1898. It is the subject of many of Graves' poems and he would often retreat there. Graves now especially wanted distance between his patriotic parents basking in the glory of their heroic son and his own awareness that most of the soldiers he knew, and almost all the officers, had suffered and died in useless battles. He felt guilty for his own survival and kept crying. At Harlech the friendship between Graves and Sassoon strengthened as they exchanged war experiences, wrote and discussed poetry. Graves unsuccessfully tried to write a novel about the war; some parts were later used in *Good-Bye to All That*.

Through Robbie Ross, Sassoon and then Graves were invited to meet Lady Ottoline Morrell whose literary salon included such famous and influential figures as Aldous Huxley, Bertrand Russell, Clive Bell and Lytton Strachey. Graves was a success but felt ill at ease. After returning to the army Sassoon and Graves shared a hut, discussed their reading, and edited each other's work.

In 1916 Graves discovered the work of the 16th-century poet John Skelton who would become his favourite poet, although for the wrong reasons. Skelton was similar to many of the other older poets Graves liked in that they were recently being rediscovered and he read him in Alexander Dyce's 1843 edition. He admired Skelton for what he thought was his plain English, satiric attitude, and, later, what he assumed was the poet's dedication to women. Actually Skelton belonged to the aureate tradition of his time and in seeking a homespun English tradition Graves misread the tone and level.[47] He edited a selection of Skelton's verse in 1927. As late as his Oxford Lectures he was still praising Skelton and in 'Tilth', written in the early 1970s, he associated himself with what he understood as the 'drab' language of Skelton in contrast to the polysyllabics of aureate writing in the 16th century and much modern jargon: 'Yet I still stand by *tilth* and *filth* and *praise*.'[48]

'The Face of Heaven', 'Oh, and Oh!' and '1915' were included in *Over the Brazier*, Graves' first volume of verse published in 1916. The title poem, which concludes the volume, has soldiers at night discussing what they will do when peace comes.

> I'd thought: 'A cottage in the hills,
>   North Wales, a cottage full of books,
>   Pictures and brass and cosy nooks
> And comfortable broad window-sills,
> Flowers in the garden, walls all white.
> I'd live peacefully and dream and write.'[49]

While descriptions of peaceful rural England which the soldier left and to which he hopes to return were a convention of Georgian war poetry, this cottage in North Wales was actually the place Graves had bought from his mother and to which he had told Sassoon they would retire and write together. The poem concludes by claiming that war had destroyed such hopes.

Over the Brazier was published by Harold Monro's Poetry Bookshop and was rapidly followed by *Goliath and David* (1917), a thin volume of which only 150 copies were printed, which included the realism of the much noticed 'A Dead Boche' intended to deflate those who wanted patriotic poetry about heroic deeds.

... he scowled and stunk
With clothes and face a sodden green,
Big-bellied, spectacled, crop-haired,
Dribbling black blood from nose and beard.[50]

'A Dead Boche', with its pure description, showed Sassoon and others how to write directly from their experience in the trenches rather than idealizing war and patriotism.[51]

The volume also included 'Careers' which lists professions that others have occupied, thus restricting his choice, until the speaker decides to be a carpenter and make a lot of money. It begins strangely with the sarcastic

Father is quite the greatest poet
That ever lived anywhere.[52]

While Graves was annoyed by questions of how he would support himself in the future, his mockery reveals feelings of competition with his father.

He found it difficult to write when in England and thought his duty was to be a good soldier and help win the war. To return the front lines he had to lie about his health. Back in France he was seen as too ill for the Front and was given other work. Just as he would later need the tensions of worshipping a demanding woman, now he needed the tensions of war to write. He was soon down with bronchitis, sent to England to recover and told to stay there, as he was on the verge of breaking down.

In England Graves, although in fragile mental condition, taught other soldiers and began cultivating a literary life which included visiting Lady Ottoline Morrell again. He was asked to contribute to an anthology of war poets and to Marsh's third anthology of Georgian poets. After overdosing on a tranquilliser and falling down a flight of steps, he was sent to a convalescent home for the shell-shocked where he worked on his third volume of poems, *Fairies and Fusiliers*.

Changed temperament

Graves continued seeing Peter during late 1916 and early 1917, but several important events happened rapidly soon afterwards. Peter, still at Charterhouse, was arrested for soliciting a Canadian soldier. This made national news when Johnstone with his family connections avoided imprisonment and was instead allowed to be treated for homosexuality by William H Rivers, a psychologist whom Graves would later consult about his own troubling war memories. Rivers' colleague Henry Head, whom Graves would often cite in future, gave evidence in Johnstone's favour. Someone sent Graves a clipping from the 2 June issue of *John Bull* in which the editor protested about Johnstone being let off. This, along with another event, in 1918, involving his friends, triggered a change in the direction of Graves' emotional life: 'Many boys recover from this perversion. I only recovered by a shock at the age of twenty-one.' During the war over 20 British officers and some 270 soldiers were court-martialled for homosexual activity.[53] Graves had a sense of survival.

Sassoon had been wounded and returned to England where he circulated a statement calling for the end of the war. As Sassoon was still in the army his action would result in court martial, which he wanted to bring publicity to his argument. Graves was stunned and blamed the pacifists who he felt influenced Sassoon and who were happy to sacrifice him for their cause. Sassoon's public refusal to fight and encouraging others to desert would lead to imprisonment and ruin his reputation; it could even have led to his execution.

By lying that the statement would not receive attention, Graves persuaded Sassoon to appear before a medical board. Graves himself kept crying when arguing that Sassoon was suffering from shell shock. Sassoon was sent to Craiglockhart War Hospital outside Edinburgh where he would be treated by William Rivers, the doctor who was also treating Graves' friend Peter Johnstone for his homosexuality. Sassoon met Wilfred Owen at Craiglockhart and showed his writings to Graves, who was impressed.[54] Sassoon and Owen became close friends and Sassoon changed Owen from writing sentimental sonnets to the realistic, experimental, at times homoerotic poetry for which he is now known. Owen, who would die fighting in France a week before the Armistice, became one of the major war poets although only a few of his verses were published during his life.

Craiglockhart was important to the war poets sent there for shell shock. Influenced by Freud, W H Rivers, the head of the psychiatric unit, believed it necessary to express rather than repress the sources of neurosis. He and his colleagues told their patients to write about their nightmares and dreams and there was a publication, *The Hydra*, for their efforts. The only poems published by Owen during his life appeared in *The Hydra*.

Graves' *Fairies and Fusiliers* (1917) was a more substantial volume than *Goliath and David* and was published commercially by William Heinemann. It includes one of his most anthologized early poems, 'Dead Cow Farm', a short mocking parody of the biblical tale of creation. 'In the beginning the first cow.' It concludes by contrasting reality to the legend. 'And the Cow's dead, the old Cow's dead.'[55] A seemingly anti-Christian poem, it could also be said to show nostalgia for what it mocks. Graves would not be the only war poet to turn against his previous faith, mock it, and remain attracted to its certainties in a time of chaos.

Robert Nichols (1893–1944), one of the Georgian poets, had fought at Loos and the Somme, suffered from shell shock and recently published his third volume of poetry *A Faun's Holiday* (1917). He would lecture on the War Poets in the USA, reappear at Oxford, and become another of Graves' ex-friends. 'To R.N.', written at Frise on the Somme, dated February 1917, rejects the sweet pastoral vision which had guided much Georgian poetry and which Nicholas continued. Graves' poem is a reply to a letter in which Nichols says he wishes Graves were with him to feed cherries to his 'faun' poems:

Cherries are out of season,
Ice Grips at branch and root,
And singing birds are mute.[56]

Like many of Graves' poems this has an ancestor, Sir Walter Raleigh's well-known reply to Marlowe's 'Passionate Shepherd to His Love'. Graves built on the shoulders of previous poets as much as T S Eliot or Pound did. Anyone with a knowledge of the work of Shakespeare, Donne, Herbert or Vaughan will often be aware of Graves' echoes that are foregrounded as part of the art and wit of his poem. For a supposed romantic he can be very classical.

Many poems in the volume are simplistic affirmations of Graves' pride in the Welch Fusiliers. 'To Lucasta on going to the Wars – for the Fourth Time' asserts that whether the cause is good or bad

> Lucasta he's a Fusilier,
>> And his pride keeps him here.[57]

This is followed by 'Two Fusiliers' in which the soldiers are bound together by having faced death and survived. In 'The Next War' as 'by the million men will drop', children play at being 'Royal Welch Fusiliers'. Instead of writing about God and country Graves writes about honour, regimental bonding and friends. Besides the Fusiliers poems there are poems dedicated to Sassoon, the dead Sorley, Nichols and other writers. Graves had told Sassoon that the volume would be dedicated to him, but instead dedicated it to his regiment. He apologized to Sassoon and said he wanted to avoid jealousy among his 'friends and lovers', Marsh, Ross, Masefield and Gosse.[58]

During June 1917 Graves began taking an interest in women. He enjoyed the company of a nurse while stationed in Sommerville, started seeing Nancy Nicholson (1899–1977), daughter of the painter William Nicholson, and soon was letting his friends know that they were wrong about his 'temperament'. This coincided with a conscious change in sexual direction after Peter's arrest, although he did not break with him until July. Graves had written Sassoon that Robert Nichols was a 'good chap' although 'his temperament is not ours'. In late 1917 he wrote to Robert Nichols saying that after the 'cataclysm of my friend Peter, my affections are running in the more normal channels'. He declared that he was not 'a confirmed homosexual'. He thought he was but it went 'no farther'.[59] Sassoon angrily noted in his diaries that he received 'apologies' from Graves for his engagement to Nancy. Graves remained in contact with Peter. Even after his marriage Graves wrote to Marsh 'that my friend Peter is publishing a little book privately' of poetry.[60]

He was just in time. Early in 1918 Graves' homosexual friends were caught up in another scandal when Noel Pemberton Billing, a Member of Parliament, published in the *Vigilante* (formerly the *Imperialist*) 'The Cult of the Clitoris', an article claiming that Robbie Ross was at the centre of a large group of pro-German homosexuals and lesbians. The article became famous when the actress Maud Allan, who had appeared as Salome in a production of Wilde's play, sued for being libelled as a lesbian. While the trial was absurd, with a doctor testifying that only a lesbian would understand the word clitoris and Billing claiming that he had been misinterpreted, Maud Allan lost the case and it ruined her career. The article, actually there were two, the first followed by a shorter one, was part of an attempt to pin the lack of success for the war on influential gays and lesbians. As unfair as the claims were, it was true that several leading pacifists such as Ross, Sassoon and some in the overlapping Lady Ottoline Morrell circle, whom Graves knew, were gay. Ross' friends included Osbert Sitwell and C K Scott-Moncrieff, the translator of Proust, as well as Graves, Sassoon and Owen. It is also true that Allan had been a success in Berlin for two years, Graves was part-German and Sassoon's first name was Siegfried, so there were reasons to be worried about the effects of the article and trial. Graves, while still in the army, married early in 1918 although he and Nancy could not at first live together. Indeed Nancy would have preferred to co-habit with Robert outside marriage and the idea was his. In *Good-bye to All That* Graves mentions an earlier interest in another woman but there is no other evidence for this.[61]

When Ross died on 5 October 1918 Graves wrote to Sassoon that he 'felt his loss more than people could suppose'.[62] Later Graves would progressively erase Ross from his history. In *Good-bye to All That* Robbie Ross is a friend, 'Wilde's literary executor, whom I had met through Siegfried and who had been very good to me', but who objected to Graves marrying Nancy because she was too young; Ross is also accused of spreading a rumour about 'negro blood in the Nicholson family'.[63] Although Sassoon wrote objecting that Graves had been unfair to Ross, in the 1957 revision 'and who had been very good to me' was omitted.[64]

Early in 1918, at the age of 23, he married Nancy Nicholson. The Nicholsons were a cultured, artistic family and Nancy's brother was the soon-to-be-famous modernist painter Ben Nicholson. Although he had often visited the Nicholsons and showed interest in Nancy's paintings, Graves had written an unpublished dream poem, 'To My Unborn Son', in which he refuses a woman's desire for intercourse to have a child but says he might change his mind. Significantly the poem is a nightmare and represents a conflict. Graves knew little about Nancy.[65]

She was 18 years old, inexperienced both sexually and in the ways of world. She was a strong feminist, aggressively unconventional and impractical. She wore her hair short in the modern style and preferred to wear smocks, trousers and neckties. Like many women she was working on a farm to support the war effort. A staunch atheist, she had not been confirmed – a source of tension with Amy Graves – saw no need to be legally married, objected to the wedding service, and immediately afterwards changed into her usual attire and, malcontent, disappeared with a bottle of champagne. Once married, she kept wishing she could be unmarried, but divorce paradoxically would be reaffirming social conventions, so she remained discontented. Her lack of conventionality affected such matters as the raising of the children, her inability to understand debt and bankruptcy, or later sharing Robert with another woman.

His marriage surprised his friends, but Ross, Marsh and Devenish attended the wedding although Sassoon refused and remained embittered for years. The marriage was probably Graves' attempt to escape from his homosexual circle of acquaintances: his relationship to women, however, would remain unusual. Even by the standards of poets and other artists his life was unconventional.

4

Nancy and Influences

1919–25

Although the Armistice was in November 1918, Graves was not demobilized until early 1919. Many of his class at Charterhouse had died in the war as had many of the poets of his generation – Wilfred Owen, Isaac Rosenberg, Charles Sorley and Rupert Brooke. Graves and Sassoon were the major survivors. The disillusionment which followed the war and the successful revolution in Russia turned many towards Socialism and Communism. Women who had worked were now demanding rights. Nancy was both a feminist and a socialist. Sassoon became an editor of the socialist *Daily Herald* for which Robert sometimes reviewed as he tried to decide what to do with his life.

At first he lived with Nancy in Wales, moving from place to place, while they played with notions of starting a communal farm preferably on Sassoon's money, but Sassoon had taken offence to a verse letter Robert sent him and the plan lacked finances. They invented a crazier scheme to live from selling dolls Nancy would make. Nancy's father rented a place on the coast at Hove in Sussex and hired a maid, for her to have her first child in comfort. Nancy, who would not give up her maiden name, agreed that all sons would be named Graves, but daughters would be Nicholsons. Jenny Nicholson was born on 6 January 1919. During February Robert, who was then stationed in Limerick, managed to return to England before the troubles in Ireland led to the suspension of demobilization.

In March Graves and Nancy travelled to Harlech and another cottage rented by her father where they would live for seven months. Amy and Alfred were mostly in London, clearing out the Wimbledon house which they planned to sell and then retire to Wales. Graves twice refused an offer of a position as a schoolteacher that Alfred obtained for him.[66] With his war bonus and savings running out and Nancy pregnant again, he reluctantly decided to take up his scholarship at St John's.

Oxford

In October 1919 Graves went up to St John's College, Oxford. The idea of being a farmer appealed to him and over the years he would plant vegetables and trees, and create gardens whenever he settled. He had played with the idea of taking a degree in Agriculture and living as a farmer, but he instead he decided, and was given permission, to do English Studies rather than

Classics. As a returning serviceman and published poet he had considerable freedom and sympathy. His unwillingness to adapt to the course of study for the degree in English and his strong feelings about what he liked and disliked amused some of his teachers. While he praised most of the faculty as individuals, he would usually speak of academics with contempt. Percy Simpson's lectures on Shakespeare's use of punctuation contributed to his own famous study of Sonnet 129 in *A Survey of Modernist Poetry*, but he disliked the poetry of Milton and the 18th-century poets. Although the lecturer thought Anglo-Saxon literature uninteresting except linguistically, Graves enjoyed the poetry, which would influence some of his later work. He was treated as an equal by his tutors and he was glad to meet people with whom he could discuss poetry. He, however, took no part in St John's undergraduate life, although his brother John also studied at St John's; the college and course in English Studies provided him with his college exhibition money and his government grant.

He was part of the post-war creative world. Starting in 1919, with William Nicholson's money, he for a few years edited *The Owl*, a quarterly literary magazine which contained illustrations of art work and paid its contributors. In 1920 he arranged to have the American poet Vachael Lindsay give a reading at Oxford, which was a success.[67] Richard Hughes, who had been at Charterhouse, co-edited *Oxford Poets 1921* with Graves. Hughes, a life-long friend, soon published *Gipsy Night* (1922), his first volume of poetry, in a limited edition of 750 badly-printed copies, followed by the more successful *The*

Sister's Tragedy and Three Other Plays (1924), and the short stories in *A Moment of Time* (1926). He was to become famous with the novel *A High Wind in Jamaica* (1929).

Peter Johnstone was also at Oxford where he had become a prize-winning poet. Although their affair never resumed Graves confessed as late as 1923 that he was emotionally upset by meeting and continuing to think about Peter. The fracture did not heal for many years, perhaps never, as Graves tried to suppress knowledge of how long his feelings continued.[68] He wrote to Marsh that he 'can't think sanely' of Peter of whom he was 'once very fond'. Graves wrote 'It will be a long while before I can meet him again without being extremely upset'.[69] (When Peter died he willed Graves his library which Graves, who had recently married his second wife, refused.)

Graves also met T E Lawrence (1888–1935) who was then a Fellow of All Souls and working on *Seven Pillars of Wisdom*. Graves showed his poems to Lawrence who made suggestions that were accepted for *The Pier-Glass* (1921), a volume dedicated to him. Graves was one of the few with whom Lawrence discussed his masochistic homosexual experience. They were both masochists who hid their shame under a facade of assertion. Lawrence would remain a close friend and useful, helping Graves when he needed money. Sassoon, who was jealous of Lawrence, continued to be upset by Graves' marriage and they seldom saw each other: he claimed that Nancy took all Graves' attention and that she had insulted Ottoline Morrell; but the real problem was jealousy as he was aware of the strong sexual undercurrent in their friendship.

Graves demanded that Sassoon accept his change in sexual orientation and also treat Nancy as a friend. Curiously Nancy was attracted to Sassoon. As Graves, when in need, had no hesitation in asking Sassoon for money there were occasional angry, even brutal, exchanges of letters for the next decade.[70]

Boars Hill

Because of his nerves Graves felt that living within Oxford was unbearable. Until 1921, he and Nancy lived nearby, at Boars Hill in Dingle, a cottage on land owned by the poet John Masefield. Edmund Blunden, a war poet whom Graves had met through Sassoon and published in *The Owl*, also studying at Oxford, was a neighbour and for a time a friend until Graves' arrogance put him off. Boars Hill attracted those, many of whom were financially secure, with interests in the arts, and soon was referred to as Parnassus; besides Graves, Robert Nichols, Blunden and Masefield, it was the home of Robert Bridges. As usual Graves enjoyed physical exercise. He and Nancy played hockey, he would bicycle to the university, and he and Nancy once bicycled to Salisbury Plain and then to Dorchester to visit Thomas Hardy whom they had earlier met at Oxford.[71]

Nancy was an artist and illustrated Graves' poems in *Treasure Box* (1920) but she was not practical. She started a small shop to support them, which was to be for poets, those with artistic inclinations and other refined customers. At first the shop attracted publicity and actually made money as Nancy delivered orders on her bicycle and locals were charmed by such eccentricities such as Graves, following his new Socialist convictions, selling similar vegetables at two prices after noticing that the well-off inevitably chose the more expensive. Soon reality and Nancy's personality had their effect and Marsh had to help financially.[72] In May 1920 while Graves' plans failed – his poems were not selling and he went into debt – his father Alfred was being honoured and entertained in Edinburgh at a Celtic Congress. Throughout much of his father's life he appeared a failure, which contributed to the son's antagonism.

Although Graves served in the shop, Nancy complained about him to customers; then in a display of foolishness she dismissed the children's nurse and was too worn out by looking after them to work.[73] Nancy lacked common sense as the nurse was devoted to the children and at times had given her own money to the couple. While it is not clear why she turned savagely against the woman and forbid her to ever see the children again, Nancy, who could be as stubborn as Graves, had her own ideas about how children should be raised; they should not be allowed meat, coffee or tea. She also was against punishment and wanted to raise children without class or other prejudices. Besides being a strong feminist and socialist, Nancy was an atheist, so there were many areas to find the nurse wanting.

Soon Graves was ill and after six months the venture failed leaving further debt. Mrs Masefield, who disapproved of Nancy and disliked the notion of a shop on Boars Hill, prevented them from selling to a larger company. They were near being declared bankrupt, which Nancy seemed to regard with indifference, until Alfred convinced Amy to help. T E Lawrence gave them some writings to sell and her father sent them £100 and settled £120 a year on Nancy.[74] Increasingly in poems Graves would blame his troubles on her. The marriage was already shaky; instead of the strong-willed, purposeful woman he seemed to need, Nancy was proving to be an impractical, scatter-brained idealist who resented her marriage. She was an early experiment in muse-creation that went wrong – too young, inexperienced, not seductive and not the right person.

Graves continued to be haunted by memories and recurring bouts of shell shock as he felt guilty for the men who had died under his command, for his own inability to have continued at the front line, and for the death of Germans who he imagined could be the cousins whose company he had enjoyed before the war. During 1921 he was close to a breakdown when a nerve specialist told him that he must stop working and put off taking his final examinations for a year.[75]

Graves left Oxford without a degree although ways would be found to enroll him for a B Litt thesis. His college exhibition and government grant ended and except for a small pension and what others gave he was left to support himself, Nancy and the children on the little he earned from writing. Sir Walter Raleigh, Head of the School of English, tried to help and could have had him appointed Professor of English at Sandhurst, but Graves turned down the offer, to the astonishment of his father who was visiting at the time and worried about the debts of the failing shop. From this time on the relationship of father and son became increasingly strained.

Graves' poetry was read favourably by John Masefield, the influential critic Edmund Gosse and the Poet Laureate Robert Bridges, but the time of the Georgians was over – the last Georgian anthologies were published in 1919 and 1922. The publication of T S Eliot's *Poems* (1919) and *The Waste Land* (1922) meant that the traditional poetic forms, metres and rhyme schemes which a poet such as Graves practised were out of fashion for decades. Even his most realistic poems still made use of poetic inversions for the sake of metre, line length or from habit. Yet it was during the 1920s that he hoped to earn his living and support his family as a poet; his lack of success contributed to the failure of his marriage and to a loss of self-confidence. Curiously the Sitwells, who were part of the new Modernism, resented what they considered Graves' success in comparison to Osbert Sitwell; 'The Death of Mercury' published in *Wheels*, 1921, satirized Graves, Squire, and others.[76] *London Mercury* published some of Graves' writings.

Marriage

Although Nancy claimed to be a modern woman and refused to adopt her husband's name, she and Graves were both virgins at the time of their marriage; he remained prudish about sexual matters. She later claimed that he was not a good lover; sex for him was a rapid release of tensions. Neither appeared to be much good for each other and it was clearly the wrong marriage for both. They made a mess of what they preached. Graves' family was far more progressive on many matters, such as birth control, than we might expect. Alfred, for example, was a friend of Marie Stopes and attended her wedding. Although both Nancy and Graves belonged to the Constructive Birth Control Society, they rapidly had four children – Jenny (1919–64), John David (1920–43), Catherine (b. 1922) and Sam (b. 1924) – and Nancy frequently complained that she was too tired for more sex.[77] Nancy's refusal to have the children baptized was a source of conflict with Amy Graves. Graves did the domestic chores, uncommon at that time. Having rejected the conventional Victorian values of the past including traditional gender roles, he lacked the time needed for his writing. Unable to support himself and his family, he required financial support from friends and Nancy's father. He often used family tensions and his sexual conflicts as motifs in poems which have an ironic content; seeming praise can be read as criticism of Nancy. His poetry was becoming his autobiography and this would continue throughout his life, although recognizing the allusions requires knowledge of his relationships.

He was psychologically a masochist with women. Influenced by his mother's claims that sex was only for procreation, the notion of physical intercourse disgusted him. It is possible to see his sudden and unexpected marriage at the age of 23 to a feminist who dressed in men's clothing and wore her hair short as a way of transferring his acknowledged homoeroticism onto a woman. Suffering from shell shock Graves took decades to recover and was subject to relapses. This was an additional reason he sought strong, commanding women although their ideas seldom worked and they could be less practical than himself. Much of his life was a complicated sexual dance which provided him with themes for poetry.

Influences

For Graves, the war, his wounding and shell shock resulted in a loss of belief in Christianity. Like others he was open to alternative visions of the world as he moved between abandoning himself to a chaotic relativism and desiring a new supportive revelation. At first he felt confused which made him seek some authoritative individual to follow. This would result in his strange relationship to Laura Riding and the search would only come to fruition with the mythology of the White Goddess.

Many of the ideas which were to become the basis of his later poetry and his notions of the White Goddess were formed around this time and reflect his readings in psychology and cultural anthropology. He had read Nietzsche during 1915 while in the trenches and this found expression in the distinction he later made between the Apollonian mind – rational, orderly and patriarchal – and that of the true poet who trusts inspiration and his muse. His rejection of bourgeois social norms inclined him towards theories about primitive society being matriarchal, sexually liberated and worshippers of a goddess.

Graves met William Rivers during the war when Rivers was treating soldiers who had nervous disorders. Rivers, an anthropologist, investigated tribal societies in India and the Pacific before studying medicine and treating shell-shocked soldiers. He introduced Graves to the ideas and works of the cultural anthropologists. Many ideas and opinions that are offered as truths in Graves' later works are based on the writings of Johann Jakob Bachofen (1815–87), Jane Ellen Harrison (1850–1928) and James Frazer (1854–1941).

The central text was Bachofen's *Mother Right: An Investigation of the Religious and Judicial Character of Matriarchy in the Ancient World* (1861). Bachofen, a Swiss who wrote in German, claimed people originally lived in a condition of sexual promiscuity since before the role of male sperm was understood in the conceiving of children, lineage was understood in terms of the mother and therefore women ruled society. It was only when the male role in conception was understood that patriarchy became dominant, as men wanted their own heirs and women became guarded property. Culture had four phases, evolving from the nomadic polyamourous, through agricultural matriarchy to a transitional Dionysian phase when patriarchy challenged matriarchy to the Apollonian role of the patriarch. In each phase the mythology reflected social practices. Bachofen's influence over the past century and a half has ranged from Friedrich Engels' claim in the 1891 edition of *Origins of the Family* that individual property rights originated in patriarchy to recent feminist claims that socialism and communalism are natural to women.

James Frazer's famous *The Golden Bough* (1890) influenced the myth of the sacrificial king in Eliot's *The Waste Land*. Frazer thought that pre-historical Europe widely practised a religious ritual based on the annual sacrifice, later symbolic, of a god-king as a way of ensuring rebirth, renewal and communal health. Communities dependent on agriculture believed that the continuation of the seasons required sacrifice to bring rebirth. Later versions of this involved sacrificial outcasts and sacrificial goats.

Graves also knew of claims that ancient rituals were the origins of drama and religion and that the original rituals were part of a matriarchal society which worshipped a goddess, a view suggested by Jane Ellen Harrison's influential *Prologomena to the Study of Greek Religion* (1903) which argued that many of the Greek festivals, especially women's festivals, developed from rituals. Harrison claimed that even earlier there was a matrilineal, matriarchal, goddess-worshipping culture. Harrison was a classical scholar who applied anthropology to the study of art, ritual and mythology, and was an important link in England to recent German scholarship and thought. She taught at Newham College, Cambridge, was part of the Bloomsbury group, and was a close friend and an influence on Virginia Woolf. In *Themis* (1912) she claimed religion had social origins and that the truth of mythology was less important than as a way of apprehending what was necessary to living.

In Graves' later development of Harrison's insights he would claim the sacrificial king began as the son and lover of the original female goddess when patriarchal ideas began to challenge matriarchy. As kings replaced priestesses, the sacred king became the symbolic sacrifice which communal health and rebirth required. Thus began the process which would lead to Christianity, Jesus' birth at the lowest point of the year and death in the spring, season of renewal. Graves' interest in matriarchal societies and religions influenced his first novel *My Head! My Head* (1925), subtitled *being the history of Elisha and the Shunamite woman; with the history of Moses as Elisha related it, and her questions put to him.*

He read Freud and his awareness of the role of the unconscious resulted in *Poetic Unreason and Other Studies* (1925). Graves decided that poetry was the result of conflict. Without conflict the imagination and poetry would lose power and he feared that undergoing a course of analysis would enfeeble his writings. Better to read up on the subject himself and keep the sources of the creative energy charged.

Although he introduced Graves to Freud's theories, Rivers had his own approach towards cures. He told Graves to write up his horrors and make poetry of them. Although Rivers expected his patients to use their writings for self-analysis he changed Graves' poetry, as can be seen by comparing *Country Sentiment* (1920) with *The Pier-Glass* (1921) and *Whipperginny* (1923).

Poetry

Some of his better known early poems are from *Country*

Sentiment, such as 'Rocky Acres' in which the landscape of Wales and the motion of the buzzard convey a sense of Graves happily self-sufficient in isolation from the complexities of the modern world and the conventions of society:

> This is the wild land, country of my choice,
> With harsh craggy mountain, moor ample and bare.
> Seldom in these acres is heard any voice
> But voice of cold water that runs from here to there
> Through rocks and lank heather growing without care.
> No mice in the hearth run, no song-birds fly
> For fear of the buzzard that floats in the sky.

This land of innocence is also a place for the gods:

> Stronghold for the demigods when on earth they go,
> Terror for fat burghers on far plain below. [78]

'Outlaws' shows that he already was identifying with 'old gods, gods of power and lust', and an imagined primitive world of myth, sacrifice and ritual:

> Banished to woods and a sickly moon,
>   Shrunk to mere bogey things,
> Who spoke with thunder once at noon
>   To prostrate kings:
>
> With thunder from an open sky

> To warrior, virgin, priest,
> Bowing in fear with a dazzled eye
> Toward the dread East – [79]

'Apples and Water' portrays a daughter innocently standing at a cottage door pitying solders marching by and saying she will fetch them water and apples. The experienced mother replies that throughout history there are soldiers and nothing can satisfy them:

> 'Once in my youth I gave, poor fool,
> A soldier apples and water;
> And may I die before you cool
> Such drought as his, my daughter.' [80]

The daughter is the result.

There are several other anthologized poems in *Country Sentiment* including 'Advice to Lovers', 'Allie' and 'A Frosty Night', but despite their acknowledgement of lust, affirmation of pre-Christian deities and claims to revolt, they are more charming than modern with their use of the pastoral, ballad rhythms and at times unnatural ordering of words to facilitate rhymes.

Some later themes are present, such as in 'The God Called Poetry', the claim to be anointed as a poet.[81] Graves was mining what was already a used-up vein of pastoral poetic diction, easy rhymes and innocent iconoclasm unlikely to shock anyone. He was surprised that reviewers found the poems slight and facile, and that the volume did not sell well. He had persuaded himself, and tried to persuade others, that the time for war poetry was over and that the reading public was now inclined towards the pastoral. He had hoped to earn money from *Country Sentiment*; it was the last volume for which he had such hopes. From now on the poetry was for himself, and he would earn money by writing prose and editing.

The Pier-Glass (1921) reveals a depressed, haunted Graves unlike the author of *Country Sentiment* (1920). The love poems tell of disappointment and demonic possession. 'The Stake', an imitation folk ballad, concludes with a 'dead heart / That the roots enfold'. 'The Pier-Glass' speaks of a haunted house and ghosts and asks 'Is there no life?'. The poems are filled with allusions to inherited sin, as in 'Reproach': 'how may a child know/ His ancestral sin?'. 'Raising the Stone' finds in ancient sacrificial monuments evidence of mankind outraging heaven by demanding 'I want, I want'.[82]

By the time of *Whipperginny* the poetry was becoming difficult, haunted by horrors, guilt and nervous breakdown. In 'A Fight to Death' two blind men fight guided by sound and touch. They quarrel over which one some woman smiled at.[83] This poetry is cleaner in diction, more up-to-date in tone. There is a stiffening of thought. The claims to disillusionment appear the result of personal experience reflected in thought. 'Song of Contrariety', about the passing lovers' intimacy after sex, concludes:

Is the person empty air,

> Is the spectre clay,
> That love, lent substance by despair,
> Wanes and leaves you lonely there
> On the bridal day?[84]

'Unicorn and the White Doe' tells of the fruitless search for lasting love and companionship:

> Vultures, rocking high in air
> By the western gate,
> Warned me with discordant cry
> You are even such as I:
> You have no mate. [85]

Disillusionment with love is common to the volume and is treated sarcastically. In 'Richard Roe and John Doe' the former being cuckolded by the latter is so affected that he is unable to think of anything grander or forming any greater revenge than becoming John Doe.[86] 'An Idyll of Old Age' ends

> Bauchis, kind soul, was palsied, withered and bent,
> Philemon, too, was ten years impotent. [87]

Although few poems from this period have lasted as well as the best from *Country Sentiment*, they are less innocent and reveal a increased complexity and toughness. The marriage to Nancy never seemed like a real love match and these poems suggest loneliness and bitterness.

A problem was that Graves was brought up in and identified himself with a tradition of writing poems influenced by the simplicity and rhythms of the ballads. His father wrote Irish folk ballads and the first poems that Robert discovered himself and loved were the old ballads 'Chevy Chace' and 'Sir Andrew Barton'.[88] Except where used ironically, as in much of W H Auden's contrasts between the pastoral world of ballads and modern industrialism and squalor, such an idiom was inappropriate to the emotions Graves needed to express. His continuing interest in this tradition can be seen from his study of *The English Ballad: A Short Critical Survey* (1927).

World's End

Graves and Nancy left Boars Hill in mid-summer 1921 and moved to World's End, a cottage in Islip, five miles north of Oxford, and would remain there until 1925. While the cottage was exactly what Nancy wanted they could not afford to buy it until Alfred, once more proving his concern for his son, convinced Amy to purchase it and rent it to them. Amy, being practical, made certain that they could not use the cottage to start another business. While they had little money and Nancy still lacked energy for painting, these were comparatively quiet years. Graves played on the local football team where he was thought too aggressive and unsportsmanlike. Nancy reminded him that they earned more than many locals, and they took pity on those unemployed ex-servicemen who went from door to door begging.[89] They even for a time housed one of their children until the girl announced she preferred being on the road with her father. For a year Graves was on the Parish Council. He was given a consolation bronze medal for a poem on sports written for the 1924 Olympic Games.

Although unable to take his final examinations due to ill-health, Graves was allowed to prepare a thesis for the B Litt, which was published before it was examined and accepted in 1926. He also wrote the first book about Lawrence, *Lawrence and the Arabs* (1927) and still later *T E Lawrence to His Biographer* (1938). It was a lasting friendship. When Graves was in financial need Lawrence sent him manuscripts and signed copies of books which he could sell. Lawrence also recommended him (and sometimes others) to producers and directors needing a scriptwriter or consultant for proposed films.

Basanta Kumar Mallik (1879–1958) was for a time a friend and a major influence on Graves.[90] A Bengali, Mallik studied philosophy in India, was a tutor to the Nepalese Prime Minister's sons, and was in 1912 sent to England to study law so as to enter government service on his return, which was delayed by the war. After Jurisprudence he studied Physical and Cultural Anthropology and became one of the literary circle at Boars Hill. After the war he spent a further five years at Oxford working towards a B Litt in Philosophy.

Graves met him in 1922. They knew the same people, including T E Lawrence, and soon became close friends arguing philosophy, playing games and sharing meals. Rivers influenced the interest in Freudian psychology found in *On English Poetry: Being An Irregular Approach to the Psychology*

Of This Art (1922) and the poems of *Whipperginny*, but Mallik turned Graves towards philosophy. Mallik's subtle metaphysics directly influenced the poems in *Mock Beggar Hall* (1924), sketches in verse and prose. *The Marmosite's Miscellany* (1925), which he published under the pseudonym Jon Doyle, included praise of Mallik in 'To M. in India':

> You with no ambition
> As I have none, nor the few friends we share,
> Except this only, to have no ambition:
> With no sure knowledge but that knowledge changes
> Beyond all local proof or local disproof[91]

Both he and Graves then held that while it was impossible to prove the truth of cultural values it was essential to be true to one's own ethics. There could be no hierarchy of values, no true religion or politics, but self-discipline and self-awareness were essential to a personal morality. Although their styles of thought were different, with Mallik's structures of argument unlike Graves' explosive insights, they shared the mixture of relativism, scepticism and intense concern with the truth of the self that was common to the period. Mallik's thesis was thought of by himself, Graves and other friends as a joint project; they were especially concerned with opposition and conflict, topics which would be central to Graves' poetry. Mallik tried to harmonize and do away with conflict by finding a Hegelian synthesis in which no one was totally wrong and in which two opposites were modified by contact with each other. In many of Graves' poems at this time there is no good or evil, but they are stages towards a synthesis which will itself change.

Graves' expounding of Mallik's thought in his own writing is a forerunner of his similar, although more intense, discipleship a few years later to Laura Riding. Mallik and Riding claimed to have created personal systems of thought and morality which transcended the scepticism common after the War. Both Mallik and Graves were concerned with domination. Mallik said one should avoid being dominated by others, a view which Graves also held. Graves' conflicts with his parents and refusal to speak to them for long periods of time were conscious attempts to reject what he considered their desire to dominate.

When Mallik returned to India in 1923 he invited T E Lawrence, Graves and Nancy to follow, but it was impractical and years later when, in 1936, Mallik returned to England Graves was already in Majorca under the influence of Laura Riding and ignored him. Although Graves mentions Mallik in *Good-bye to All That* he gets the facts of his life wrong and claims – such stereotypes are themselves typical of Graves – that as an Indian his thought reached a dead-end, which was intended as a contrast to Laura.

Virginia and Leonard Woolf were more acquaintances than friends. Graves began publishing poetry pamphlets, starting with *The Feather Bed*, with their Hogarth Press in 1923; *Mock Beggar Hall* (1924) and *The Marmosite's Miscellany* (1925) followed. He did not meet the Woolfs in person until 1925 when he arrived at their house badly dressed, talked too much about Nancy, stammered, overstayed his welcome, and was thought by Virginia more someone who needed charity than a real poet.[92] He was not a Bloomsbury person, but the Woolfs continued to publish his critical essays, *Contemporary Techniques of Poetry: a Political Analogy* (1925), *Another Future of Poetry?* (1926) and *Impenetrability: or the Proper Habit of English* (1926).

Graves' poetry and his early *On English Poetry* (1922) had been favourably noticed by John Crowe Ransom, the leader of the 'Fugitives' at Vanderbilt University in Nashville, Tennessee. The importance of *On English Poetry* was the argument that value depends on the range of associations brought to mind by the words of a poem. Later critics would use such terms as 'ambiguity', 'complexity', and 'levels of meaning', often resorting to difficult jargon, to explain that poetry often uses overlapping patterns of implied resonances to create associations that go beyond statements.

Ransom was a good poet himself, founder of the literary journal *Fugitives*, a regional American branch of the Modernist movement. Its associates included the poet-critic Allen Tate and it was one of the sources of the New Critics in America. The Fugitives lamented the industrialized modern world being imposed on the South by the North and they idealized a rural yet cultured regional way of life destroyed by the American Civil War. Such reactions to modern mass society and the role of science in industrialization were common to Modernism. Ransom initiated a correspondence with Graves and sent him copies of his books.

Although like almost everyone else after the war Graves went through a socialist phase, he was apolitical and conservative; he wrote about himself and was sceptical of organized politics. While he disliked Modernist poetry he was similar to many Modernists such as late Yeats, Eliot, and D H Lawrence in distrusting mass democracy, hating industrialization and in his attraction to the myths and rituals of the past.

The marriage between Nancy and Graves was unhappy as he needed more intellectual conversation. Nancy, who was often ill, resented the time spent on children and wanted to work at her art. She felt neglected and needed a companion. They seemed only happy when a third person was present. During this period Graves was usually in dire financial straits and began to see that his attempt to earn a living as a poet was a failure; indeed he seemed unable to earn much as any sort of writer. He reluctantly thought of teaching, but several attempts to find a post ended in failure.

He was already preparing himself to become the Muse-haunted poet of his later decades. He needed to be dominated by a woman and enjoyed performing such traditional female roles as preparing and cooking food, serving the partner in bed, and following the partner's authority on financial matters and where to live. He had intellectually prepared himself through readings in the mythology proclaimed by Jane Harrison and James Frazer claiming a pre-history of the world before it fell into patriarchy and Christianity. A domineering mother, dislike of school bullies, the horrors of the war, Nancy's feminist arguments, the Russian Revolution, his shell shock, the mistreatment of the returning soldiers and his own confused sexual urges left him ready for a social and cultural revolution in which women ruled. Nancy was not a commander. She was not practical, had limited ambitions, was often ill with a thyroid deficiency, and seemed more trapped in her marriage than able to become Graves' leader. He needed another Amy, someone who knew and insisted upon what was right and wrong, but the desired values would be in keeping with the post-war rebellion against Victorianism, the opposite of those Amy held. He was confused about his life, sexual drives, how to earn a living; he needed someone who could provide clarity or whom he could successfully invite to take on that role. Laura Riding was instinctively such a person, and given the chance it suited her for almost a decade and a half.

5

Laura and
Good-bye to All That

1926–9

In 1925 Graves and Nancy invited Laura Riding (1901–91), an American poet and self-proclaimed prophet, to come to England the following year and then accompany them to Egypt where Graves had been appointed for three years as the first Professor of English at the new University of Cairo. The appointment required influence as he lacked qualifications and was not emotionally stable: it would be the last time he would work at anything other than writing.

Siegfried Sassoon had first been invited to accompany them to Egypt, but wisely declined; instead a rather different trio developed. Laura was from a New York Austrian Jewish immigrant family. Early in life she was recognized as being very bright but subject to hysterical temper-tantrums. She often became so excited that she fainted. While studying at Cornell University she was committed to a mental asylum for a time during a breakdown. Her brother also spent time in an asylum.[93]

While still a child she studied Marx as her father hoped that she would lead America to socialism: instead she expected to save the world through her involvement in culture. She studied at Cornell from 1918 to 1920, where she began writing poetry and married (1920) and later divorced (1925) Louis Gottschalk, a history instructor, whom she followed to Louisville, Kentucky, where he had a teaching position. On the make but unable to make it in the USA, she lied about her family but her pretences were betrayed by her voice which sounded foreign. Her undeniable talent and intelligence were insufficient for her ambition; she understood that her way upward depended on men. She had been awarded a Fugitive poetry prize (1924), failed to win Allen Tate from his future wife, failed to take over the Fugitives, and during 1925 was for a time the sidekick in Greenwich Village of the homosexual poet Hart Crane. Graves was impressed by 'The Quids', her witty prize-winning satire on the artistic world, inquired about her from Ransom, and soon a correspondence developed which led to the invitation to join them, at their expense, in Egypt.

Laura had the energy, practical ability and literary interests that Nancy lacked, while providing Graves with a bed partner. They consciously became a threesome as Nancy happily let her become Graves' lover. Such a scenario must have been on Graves' and Nancy's minds as the relationship was foreshadowed in *The Shout*, finished in 1927, a weird short story about a couple that becomes a trio. (It was made into a horror film in 1978 with Jerzy Skolimowski directing Alan Bates, Susannah York and John Hurt. Tim Curry takes the role of Robert Graves.) Graves' life had begun to alter radically during 1926. He needed some new direction and seldom saw his former friends. Once Laura was on the scene and the three travelled to Egypt, Graves and Nancy would return transformed, their marriage redefined as they lived in open defiance of social convention while new friends replaced those they left behind. Laura changed his life. '1926 was yesterday, when the autobiographical part of my life was fast approaching its end.'[94]

After modelling his verse on folk songs and ballads, Graves now changed the manner of his poetry. Following the failure of *John Kemp's Wager* (1925), a ballad opera which was only performed once, his poetry started to have a new satiric edge, as can be seen in 'Alice' from *Welchman's Hose* (1925). It was time for a change. His poetry of the 1920s did not sell and received much less favourable attention than the war volumes. He also changed publisher; after quarrelling with William Heinemann his next volumes, beginning with *Country Sentiment*, were published by Martin Secker. Graves was still an admirer of such poets as Walter de la Mare, John Masefield and W H Davies, and disliked how fashions in poetry had moved on. While critical of many modernist poets, Laura saw herself as part of the avant-garde and led Graves in a more contemporary direction. He never became a modernist writer of obscure,

difficult verse, but under Laura's criticisms he eliminated older
mannerisms while addressing such themes as sexual desire and
resentment that he formerly treated indirectly if at all. During
1926–7 his poetry became more infused with thought, more
paradoxical, skeptical, aggressive, tougher. His first major
poem, 'The Cool Web', a 16-line extended sonnet, shows this
new direction his poetry would take:

> There's a cool web of language winds us in,
> Retreat from too much joy or too much fear:
> We grow sea-green at last and coldly die
> In brininess and volubility.[95]

The Cairo professorship sounded good, with only two
lectures a week; amusingly, the university occupied a former
harem. He would have a proper place in the world in keeping
with his parents' expectations. Sassoon paid for a car, sent
from England, and they were going to a place where they had
connections. Graves' half-brother Richard, who was a married
diplomat in Egypt, tried to help, as did his half-sister Molly,
who also lived in Cairo, but the months there were unhappy.

Nancy pined for England and Laura was bored. The
children became ill. Although Graves had little teaching to do,
he hated his job and Egypt; he seemed determined to upset
the British community by appearing with Laura at university
events without Nancy. He resigned his professorship before
finishing the first of his contracted three years, and the trio
returned to England where Laura took over the bed and

began the formation of a cult of followers while Nancy lived separately, painted and designed dresses. Soon Graves would desert her and their children, although it would be almost two decades before she was willing to divorce him.

Back in England there were financial problems and they sold the car. T E Lawrence once more helped, this time with a first edition of *The Seven Pillars of Wisdom* which sold for £330.[96] When Lawrence no longer wanted *Revolt in the Desert* (1926), a shortened version of *The Seven Pillars of Wisdom*, kept in print, Graves was approached by Cape to write a book on the topic. The idea was to keep out an American author whom Lawrence disliked. The plans were originally to write a children's book in under two months, but the manuscript grew as Graves sent Lawrence, then in India, his writing for comment. The result was a large, highly laudatory book, *Lawrence and the Arabs* (1927) for which Graves was paid an advance of £500; it sold well, made money, and remained in print for years.[97] From now on he would earn large sums of money which would rapidly disappear thanks to his aristocratic ways. With some of the money he bought an old printing press with the idea of starting his own publishing house, the Seizin Press.

At first Nancy remained in the country in her father's house in Cumberland while Graves and Laura looked for a place in London; for a time they settled in Ladbroke Square. By now Graves had openly become Laura's lover. Nancy seemed unbothered, but Laura planned to get rid of her and the children by sending them to America.[98] Graves and Laura went to Austria for three months where they met his disapproving parents, and returned to England where Nancy no longer wanted to share any home with Laura.[99]

In 1927 Graves rented an apartment in Laura's name at 35A St Peter's Square, Hammersmith, London, and they became part of a partying bohemia. Whereas Nancy liked the country, Laura's natural milieu was an urban bohemia of artists, intellectuals, sexual freedom and competing over-sized egos. She no longer pretended to be Nancy's close friend. Graves thought her a goddess, and he demanded his acquaintances accept his evaluation. Soon he had fewer friends, many of whom he would not hear from again until years later when he and Laura separated.[100] While Laura spoke of the need for honesty and directness, she was herself devious and manipulative; he was increasingly tactless, ensuring the fraying of old friendships with those, such as Sassoon, who had helped him in the past.[101]

Graves and Laura met others who in coming years would be part of their circle – the poet and painter Norman Cameron and his painter friend John Aldridge. Len Lye was a brilliant unconventional New Zealander who had studied rituals in Samoa, made animated films, and like them enjoyed social dancing.[102]

Graves was trying to rid himself of his puritanical, middle-class upbringing, and feelings of guilt and failure. 'The Reader Over My Shoulder' is himself, his conscience, his past:

For you in strutting, you in sycophancy,
Having played too long this other self of me,
   Doubling the part of judge and patron.[103]

While trying to separate 'the damned confusion of myself
and you' and assert a new life, he had earlier tried to follow
Mallik's warning against dominance by others, but he became
dominated by Mallik. Now, asserting his independence, he
became Laura's puppet. He needed a puppet master. They
would work together, either co-authoring books or submit-
ting their work to each other for editing and approval; in this
arrangement Graves had the talent but she had the opinions.
She co-authored Graves' influential *A Survey of Modernist
Poetry* (1927), apparently the first time 'Modernist' literature
was called such, and *A Pamphlet Against Anthologies* (1928).
After a period of sharing, Laura became dominant.

   Late in 1927 Graves bought a barge, the *Avoca*, for Nancy
and the children, which was followed by a trip to Paris for Laura
to visit Gertrude Stein whom she admired and imitated. They
returned to London in June 1928. The children moved to the
barge but Nancy at first ignored it until on a visit to London
she decided to stay as Graves and Laura were neglecting the
children who were ill. He then bought a more comfortable
barge, the *Ringrose*, for Nancy and the children, but Laura
was becoming bored with him.[104] She wanted a new, younger,
more attractive admirer.

   Enter Geoffrey Phibbs (1900–56), a good-looking,
charming 28-year-old unsuccessful poet, who wrote admiringly

to Laura from Dublin. His *Withering of the Fig Leaf* (1927) was published by Hogarth Press and then suppressed by Phibbs because of its anti-Catholicism. He also published with Hogarth Press, using the name R Fitzurse, *It was Not Jones* (1928), in an edition of 500 of which 290 were eventually pulped. Laura sent Graves to interview him and soon Geoffrey wanted to move to London. He was in an unhappy marriage with Norah McGuinness, an older woman who had a fling with the writer David Garnett. Geoffrey is said to have suggested that he and Garnett and their wives become a foursome, an invitation which Garnett refused. Norah accompanied Geoffrey to London in February 1929, and was soon parked in a hotel by Laura and told to stop crying. Geoffrey became part of what Laura now called the 'Holy Circle'. Laura believed that she had magical powers and he was told to burn his clothes, made to write 'Seizin Press' in his books which Norah had forwarded, and various cabalistic signs were used and astrological charts formed to show that his past was over and he was made new. Soon there was a sexual foursome with the men changing partners according to Laura's wishes.[105] William Nicholson, Nancy's father, objected to the arrangement, refused further financial help, and commented 'that now the Turks have abandoned polygamy, Robert ... decided to take it up.'[106]

Laura and Graves were part of a set at the time well known for unconventionality. Lucie Brown, a fashion designer, had married a homosexual and afterwards had a bisexual boyfriend who attended the Great Ormond Street orgies held by Cedric

Morris and Lett Haines, two men who lived together. John Aldridge (1905–83) and Norman Cameron (1905–53) were bisexual and both familiar with the drug den and brothel at Ham Common, Richmond, which Laura and Graves would later visit.[107] With Laura's aid, Graves had become everything his mother hated.

Geoffrey was more inhibited. He was often impotent when it was his turn to bed Laura as he felt sorry for Graves and Nancy whom he came to see as her victims. (Laura had bad luck with her lovers. Hart Crane, who she did not know was a homosexual, had been impotent with her before she left for England.) It took only a month for Geoffrey to have enough of her. She once hysterically locked herself in a lavatory for eight hours because he correctly claimed to be taller than her.[108] On 1 April he quietly disappeared for France where his wife Norah was now studying painting. Laura became hysterical, blamed Graves and sent him to Ireland in search of Geoffrey, then a letter arrived from France; the postmark suggested Geoffrey might be in Rouen. Laura, Nancy and Graves found his hotel address and left immediately for Rouen where they demanded that Geoffrey and Norah discuss the situation, made cabalistic signs, and invited Norah to make it a fivesome, which she refused. When Geoffrey said he would stay with Norah, Laura became hysterical, threw herself on the floor, and had to be carried out by two waiters.[109] Nancy, Laura and Graves returned to London.

Then Geoffrey returned to Ireland where he began receiving objects sent by Laura with cabalistic signs. Nancy travelled to

Ireland but failed to make him return. Geoffrey visited David Garnett to ask for advice, and was told to stay away from them, but when Geoffrey sent a telegram telling of his decision, Laura demanded Graves bring him back, and he threatened to kill Geoffrey if he did not travel to London with him.

Attempted suicide

Arriving on the evening of 26 April 1929 Geoffrey refused to apologize to Laura who claimed that he had mistreated her and the Circle. The next morning the quarrel resumed with Geoffrey telling Laura that nothing she could say would change his mind. Laura left the room, reappeared claiming that she had drunk Lysol, a poison, and when that seemed to have no effect she jumped out of a window on the third floor, melodramatically shouting 'Goodbye, chaps'.

What happened next is confusing but Graves jumped after her from a window on the staircase a half storey lower. Nancy telephoned Graves' sister Rosaleen, a doctor, and called for an ambulance. Laura was taken to a hospital where she was found to have a broken pelvis, a bent spinal cord, and four crushed lumbar vertebrae. Graves blamed himself for Laura's injuries. Geoffrey told the police what happened.[110]

After her attempted suicide Laura was hospitalized for months and Graves was interviewed by the police on suspicion of attempted murder. Attempted suicide was a crime and Laura, an alien, was likely to be deported. Graves used his contacts with Edward Marsh, then secretary to Winston Churchill,

Chancellor of the Exchequer, to prevent her prosecution. It is revealing of how far Graves had travelled from his earlier puritanism that he accused the police of taking 'an old-fashioned moral view ... They blame it all on Laura and think that G. was the innocent hero decoyed into a den of perverts'. Meanwhile Geoffrey and Nancy were living together with her children on the barge. They suggested renewing the Holy Circle but Graves, seeing a chance to have Laura to himself, rejected the proposal, and wrote to Nancy saying that 'I love Laura beyond everything thinkable and that has always been so'. He told Nancy 'The children are yours'. Meanwhile Graves set about slandering his rival, claiming that Geoffrey, desiring Nancy, had threatened to throw Laura out the window.[111] Such inventions and demonisation of rivals would become a standard part of Graves' future repertoire.

This was his chance to have Laura to himself. There would be no more Holy Circle, he would desert his wife and children and take Laura away. Attempts by Nancy or Geoffrey to make up were rebuffed and Graves did what he could to prevent Geoffrey from finding employment.[112] Like Laura, he could be childish: he even refused to return Geoffrey's books until forced to by a court order. He sent a bill demanding reimbursement for the clothes he had given him after Laura burnt Geoffrey's possessions during the initiation ritual.

Graves and Nancy were from well-known families and the parties and couplings in Hammersmith were the stuff of London gossip. Although some sympathized with Graves, others felt he had long been rushing towards disaster. There is evidence from her writings, especially the poem '1927' and her diaries, that Laura was dissatisfied with her life and was contemplating suicide before the break-up with Geoffrey; even her melodramatic farewell 'Goodbye, chaps' before jumping from the window was likely planned.[113]

Good-bye to All That

A month after Laura's attempted suicide Graves began working intensively on *Good-bye to All That* (1929), supposedly his autobiography until then. Both a declaration of his new start in life and a way to earn money to support their life abroad, it was one of a number of autobiographical books, such as Herbert Read's *In Retreat* (1925), T E Lawrence's *Seven Pillars of Wisdom* (1926), Edmund Blunden's *Undertones of War* (1928), R H Mottram's *Ten Years Ago* (1928), and Sassoon's *Memoirs of a Fox Hunting Man* (1928) and *Memoirs of an Infantry Officer* (1930), written by young men who had been in the Great War.[114] *Memoirs of an Infantry Officer* portrayed Sassoon's now embittered relationship with Graves under the name 'David Cromlech', a fad-influenced crank to whom he had been attracted.

Good-bye to All That was a cultural history of the period in its movement from the restrictions and bullying of the pre-war era to the horrors of the war and the confusions and revolt that followed. Graves' conflicted life included a famous public school, homoeroticism, sexual repression, the Georgians, friendships with other war poets, studying English at Oxford, and awareness of Freud, Frazer, W H Rivers, psychology, cultural anthropology, socialism and feminism. Except for some concluding allusions to the Geoffrey Phibbs affair and Laura's jump and injury, the narrative avoids discussing the role Laura had and the experimental pairings she brought about. In the 'Epilogue' to the 1929 edition Graves' relationship to Laura and Nancy is expressed as 'a unity to which you and I pledged our faith and she her pleasure'.[115] This is followed by several paragraphs which are obscure unless you already know what happened.

Autobiographies written by the young during the late 1920s rejected Victorian values and saw a continuation between the class-ridden England of their schooling and life in the army, with their teachers being replaced by snobbish, bullying officers and the national leaders sacrificing the young in a hopeless war for the sake of false ideals. They reflect a generational conflict in which the elders continued to live by beliefs that the war made foolish. *Good-bye to All That* was widely reviewed, even making the front page of British newspapers, and became a best-seller. It remains a modern classic as a portrait of British middle-class puritanical rigidities; for its revelations of the homosexuality, hypocrisy, anti-intellectualism and lack of educative purpose in a famous public school; and for its tight-lipped disillusioning record of what it was like to be a soldier during the First World War. The famous battles which left many soldiers dead and wounded are shown to have been badly prepared and unlikely to succeed. Equipment and training are poor, long marches with heavy packs are undertaken for no purpose, while the shelling and knowledge of probable death rapidly result in nervous breakdowns, refusals to follow orders, and suicide. The government, newspaper editorials and civilians seem indifferent or blind to the toll taken on the soldiers. Although Graves never says so, the horrors of the war reveal the falseness of the society, its leaders and its values.

The England to which Graves and other soldiers return seems alien, having little to do with or for them. The effects of his damaged lung, his shell-shocked nerves, and his inability to settle down are in the foreground of a picture which also includes a post-war England in which educational qualifications are once more necessary for employment while jobless veterans tramp up and down the country seeking subsistence. The returning soldiers are aware of events in Russia and hope for revolution in England. Graves does not devote much space to the problems of post-war England but the reader is conscious of a fracture between those who had fought and the reassertion of class and other snobberies. Meanwhile a new generation, represented by Nancy, have other concerns, such as the rights of women, and cannot understand what the soldiers went through.

The 'Good-bye' of the title was a 'Good-bye' to the pre-Laura world, a history he now rejected. He assumed that his life from now on would exist in a separate, private space, a world in which Laura would be his guide and purpose. The autobiography, as can be seen from the introductory poem by Laura, and the 'Dedicatory Epilogue to Laura Riding' which concludes the 1929 edition, is meant to show what he was leaving behind. Graves' parents objected to such increasing unconventionality and his father published a quibbling but accurate reply as *To Return to All That* (1930).

Graves often uses the term 'caricature' for such situations as the priggish poet's new boxing ability being feared by those who bully him. Much of what he records is ironic, such as his father, famous for educational reform and a school inspector, sending him to inappropriate schools, or Graves' joining the army to avoid going to Oxford, or his acceptance as an officer although he was a pacifist who had avoided officer training. Similar incongruities are true of military life with its snobberies, its officers playing polo near the front line, the luxurious meals some officers enjoy, the lies the government and newspapers tell about the war, and the quiet but terrible irony that after all the pain and death nothing changes. Graves keeps being sent to the same places: the front line remains as before but the places have been totally destroyed.

The pointless repetition of the fighting is shown in the many brave actions that are not rewarded with decorations because the captured area is later lost and the victory is recorded as a defeat. Even official reports of Graves' death prove false and he soldiers on. His acceptance of a gentleman's code of honour and his standing by the regiment does instill discipline and courage, but it dooms him to going along with what he regards as useless orders that result in senseless deaths.

Laura does not appear in the narrative as she is outside what he is leaving: she claimed that the past was over and she and her followers existed outside history. When *Good-bye to All That* was republished in 1959, Graves revised the style and deleted the introductory poem and 'Dedicatory Epilogue', removing indications of the original cause of the book. The later version seems a more conventional story about the pains of public-school life, the horrors of the war and the difficulties of adjusting to life afterwards.

The book was meant to earn money so Graves and Riding could leave England, and 120,000 words were rapidly dictated to Jane Lye, the wife of his friend Len.[116] It was started in May 1929, finished in August and published in November. Controversy resulted from the dismissive tone about Charterhouse, the conduct of the war and Graves' attitude. Many facts are wrong, and few can be trusted. For example, most of what he wrote about Basanta Kumar Mallik's background and politics is nonsense. Sassoon wrote to Graves, 'There are no *understatements* in your book.' Threats of lawsuits by those who had seen advance copies resulted in some last-minute changes, mostly deletions, even inclusion of a erratum slip. The complete, original, unabridged 1929 edition was not published until edited and restored by Graves' nephew Richard Perceval Graves in 1995.[117]

That Graves had dictated *Good-bye to All That*, invented details and reworked earlier attempts at autobiographically-based fiction resulted in an energetic, rapid, anecdotally varied and entertaining story, which combines narrative momentum with the abruptness of speech. The scenes with their exaggerated stereotypical behaviour are staged comic turns. The paragraphs are a model of how to build an opening theme to a striking conclusion. The one beginning 'I find it very difficult to love the French here' ends 'every British hospital train, the locomotive and carriages of which had been imported from England, had to pay a £200 fee for use of the rails on each journey they made from railhead to base'.[118] Lytton Strachey, appearing before a military panel as a conscientious objector, says in a falsetto voice that if a German tried to rape his sister '"I would try to get between them".'[119] In contrast to such humour are the many portraits of rebels, such as Rodakowski, Mallory, Lawrence and Sassoon, who heroically refuse to accept conventions.[120]

The book is full of incident, tales, opinions, life; there is a rapid alternation and variety of tones and moods. Amusing tales (6 June) of a few days billeted in a town behind the lines ('Troops are forbidden to bomb fish. By order of the Town Mayor') are followed by the grotesque (9 June):

At my feet was the cap he had worn, splashed with his brains. I had never seen human brains before; I had somehow regarded them as a poetic figment. One can joke with a badly-wounded man and congratulate him on being out of it. One can disregard a dead man. But even a miner can't make a joke that sounds like a joke over a man who takes three hours to die after the top part of his head has been taken off by a bullet fired at twenty yards range. Beaumont, of whom I told you in my last letter, was also killed. He was the last unwounded survivor of the original battalion, except for the transport men. He had his legs blown against his back.[121]

This leads to a scene (24 June) in which the senselessness of war is shown through Chaplinesque comedy. Graves is billeted in a town which was 'taken and retaken eight time last October' and is now mostly destroyed and deserted by civilians. Graves and a sergeant-major discover a garden with blackcurrant bushes which they start eating ignoring each other, then remember their dignity, salute, feign leaving, and return in a few minutes each hoping to have the blackcurrants to himself. They once more stop, salute, pretend to be admiring flowers, and go away. This time, however, the bushes are stripped clean by some privates.

Graves rapidly moves from the macabre to the senti-mental and then to the unjust without changing his seemingly objective tone. A new officer finds two rats at night fighting over a severed hand. 'This was thought a great joke'. In the next paragraph, describing a suicidally dangerous night patrol for which he volunteered, Graves and a sergeant find a fat German lying on his back humming the 'Merry Widow' waltz. Graves decides not to kill him. When he manages to return safely to his lines he is accused of '"cold feet"'.[122]

Rather than endless details of the horrors of trench warfare, the book is filled with the variety of life. There are stories about French prostitutes, men killing their unfaithful wives, inter-regimental tensions, and the hatred between the British and the French who they were supposedly defending. The officers and common soldiers supposedly go to different whore houses. The instructor showing how to handle bombs (i.e. hand grenades) with care is blown up during the demonstration. 'To illustrate the point he rapped it against the edge of the table. It killed him and another man and wounded twelve others more or less severely.' [123]

When *Good-bye to All That* is re-read in the light of R P Graves' detailed biographical research for *The Assault Heroic* it seems as much an example of self-deception as self-revelation. Robert used his autobiography as a way of creating a past which was only partly true. He did not, for example, acknowledge the important place his father and family had in the literary world, the influence of his father on making him a poet, nor the extent to which his father had tried to further his literary career. The portrait of his days at Charterhouse is distorted. Much of his time there Graves was happy, and he encouraged his younger brother to apply. He played down the strength of his homosexual feelings and his patriotism and religiosity during the war. Sassoon wrote to Graves complaining at the falseness of some statements and Sassoon and Blunden annotated a copy of *Good-bye to All That* now in the Berg Collection of the New York Public Library showing up Graves' many errors, some of which were no doubt intentional.

The fact of its being misleading does not detract from *Good-bye to All That* as literature. Graves claimed that a writer has the right to invent if he keeps to the spirit of the work, a view he often expressed of the writer's imagination being superior to mere rationality. With *Good-bye to All That* the problem is not merely that he edited and invented history to make a better story; he often misleads about the past in ways that might be thought dishonest. Throughout his life Graves would continue to assume that whatever he wanted to believe was true; he had little sympathy with contrary opinions, especially when supported by evidence.

Good-bye to All That became a warm-up for the historical novels Graves would write in Deià. Although each would be the story of an individual they were also about an unjust world, the snobberies and ambitions of an incompetent ruling class, the end of empire and the importance of honour to moral survival and its uselessness in practice. There was a similar alteration of battle scenes and the personal in narrating the end of an era.

6

Deià, Good-bye Robert

1929–39

B y the time reviews of *Good-bye to All That* reached Graves, he and Laura were living in Majorca. Gertrude Stein told them that Majorca was Paradise if you could stand it; they disliked Palma because of the many resident British and Germans: instead they settled in the mountainous village of Deià. It was beautiful and small with perhaps 300 inhabitants, and always had a few foreign artists renting its stone houses or living in a pension. It was almost completely isolated; a local bus went in the morning from Deià to Palma and returned in the evening with any post. The only electricity was locally generated, went off by ten in the evening, and suitable lightbulbs still had to be made by hand well into the 1950s. Even in the 1960s when Kingsley Amis visited Deià, he found it perfect for a writer, citing its lack of tourists and nightclubs, its lack of telephones and lack of parking space for cars at the beach. There was still one bus a day to and from Palma.[124]

Laura and Graves first lived outside the village in Casa Salerosa, which had an excellent view but was damp and cold; the winters were terrible. They thought they bought land to build a two-storey house, Canelluñ, on the opposite, sunny, side of the village although under Spanish law it was illegal for them to own property so close to the sea shore. Juan Marroig Mas, usually known as Juan Gelat, the man who sold them the land, kept ownership in his name. Laura, who liked to control people, liked domineering men and Gelat knew that she would agree to what he suggested and Graves would pay for it. Graves was like the emperors of the novels he would write – ruled by women attracted to other men.

Graves spent several years building Canelluñ, preparing the land for growing fruit and vegetables, and building roads, including a path to a beach. He moved in during spring 1932, having lived for a time at another house, C'an Pa Bo, while keeping Casa Salerosa for visitors.[125] Over a decade later he would need to repurchase the land; by then he was less innocent and knew Ricardo Sicre (a Catalonian whom Graves helped get to New York where he became wealthy) who had the property legally included within the village boundaries instead of on the prohibited sea coast. Canelluñ became the centre of Graves' life, except for eight years of wartime wandering, until his death. He bought other properties as guest houses for friends visiting Deià and he would still need to purchase some of his land for a third time when Gelat's widow claimed ownership.

Leaving England for Majorca seems natural now, but then it was more an act of desperation than just following the sun. Laura initially did not want to go to Spain, but by 1929 Graves' life was a mess. Since leaving the army he had quarrelled with friends, made a bad marriage, had four children whom he would not support, and become part of a *menage à trois* which expanded to an unsuccessful *menage à quatre*, so unsuccessful that the deranged woman he loved had tried to commit suicide, which lead to Graves being suspected of attempted murder. His poetry during the 1920s had bad reviews and poor sales. Even Nancy preferred Geoffrey Phibbs and was living with him. By leaving Nancy and the children he was making a clean break with the past, including his disapproving, hectoring parents, saying *Good-bye to All That*, a book which, like *Lawrence and the Arabs*, was a financial success and which would be followed by best-selling novels. The penny-pinching time was over.

It was less clean a break than he claimed. Showing his anger and refusal to accept the usual rules of behaviour while claiming that he and Laura were pursuing a more honest way, he took Nancy's silver cutlery and her mother's chairs, which he refused to return. He claimed that Nancy and the Nicholsons owed them to Laura for their past insults.[126] Such childishness, lack of conventional ethics and insistence that others agree with him became typical of his behaviour. Behind it was his determination not to be dominated by anyone except those he chose to influence him, and, ultimately, his continuing battle with his parents, especially his domineering mother, a fight which he transferred to his father. Whereas his relationship with his distant but scolding mother mixed love and hate, he could hate his helpful and comradely father without confusion.

Jonathan Cape wanted a successor to *Good-bye to All That*; instead Graves provided *But It Still Goes On* (1931), a miscellany including newspaper articles, bits of a journal, short stories and a bad but self-revealing play in which the hero is a figure representing Graves and the villain is his father, who is accused of helping his son's career and giving him money in financial emergencies as a way to dominate him. Graves' hatred of his father in this work is so intense as to be irrational. There is also a complaining interview with God.

The small world that he and Laura inhabited was something they could control. For seven years they would act like king and queen of a tiny circle, within the society of foreigners in Deià. Graves and Laura claimed that they purposefully limited their friends, but while they were always making judgments there were few people who shared their interests.

Although he would permit no criticism of Laura, Graves knew that she could be become irrational, and that there was insanity in her family. The powerful short lyric 'Sick Love' which introduces *Poems 1929* shifts rapidly from echoes of Canticles, 'O Love, be fed with apples', to allusions to 'paranoiac fury' while praising the woman as 'Exquisite in the pulse of tainted blood':

Be warm, enjoy the season, lift your head,

Exquisite in the pulse of tainted blood,
That shivering glory not to be despised.[127]

As can be seen from *Ten Poems More* (1930, composed in Deià but published by Hours Press, Paris), Laura could do no wrong; he was already creating a mythology with characteristics later found in his White Goddess.

Laura believed she was a prophet meant to lead followers who would save the world. She offered no message beyond herself; what she said was right and her followers were to worship her and give her presents in acknowledgement. When visitors did not give her the presents that she wanted she became angry.[128] She gave the group and her work various names which kept changing; she said she was working on projects that would redefine words, thought, everything, projects with which her followers were to help. Graves worshipped her and demanded that any visitors should as well. Like Nancy, she was often ill, expected Graves to do the domestic work and serve her, even roll her cigarettes, and for a period of six years refused him sex by claiming she was now on a higher plane of purity; sex belonged to the past. Claiming sex was disgusting, she tried to prevent guests from having any privacy, demanding that bedroom doors be left open.[129] She implied that she had magical powers – themes echoed in Graves' poetry of the time; she was also malicious, spread rumours, admitted no faults, and tried to dominate others. She dressed exotically in Mallorcan clothes, wore much glittering jewellry, spoke with affected emphasis on words, stared others in the eye until they blinked and when speaking pointed a finger towards them.

Graves, being inferior, was allowed to have mistresses. This, however, is cloudy territory, the subject of hints and later memories. It is said that in 1931 Graves made a German, Elfrieda Faust, pregnant and Laura forced her to have an abortion. Miranda Seymour thinks this unlikely but her reasons are not convincing.[130] Laura encouraged Graves' lapses to keep him under her control; she wrote that in this new era women would become the judges and men the judged.[131] Decades later she would claim that Graves' mythology of the White Goddess was an obscene distortion of herself and her thought, but the views she professed during the 1930s were similar to his own. She played up to his need to love, deify and be humiliated by both believing herself divine and by seeing in his emotional and sexual demands an example of how males create fantasies about the objects of their desire – fantasies which are central to the tradition of love poetry that Graves followed. Such fantasies were necessary to how men created.

Friends

By 1932 a small group including Norman Cameron and Elfrieda Faust, John Aldridge and Lucie Brown, and Tom Matthews and his new wife Julie were often in Deià, helping Graves and Laura in their various projects. Laura always seemed to be working on something immense which would change the world, but whatever it was called, and it kept changing, it was impractical and unpublishable.

Life took on a routine. During the warm weather Graves and others, but not Laura, would go to the cala, the small pebbled beach. Afternoons would be spent writing, editing and reading. In the late afternoon the group would meet at a café and have a drink while awaiting the bus returning from Palma with the mail. In the evenings there were dinners and parties at which Graves sang, told stories, invented games, played bridge or listened to music. Both he and Laura enjoyed dancing. People drifted off and were replaced by others, including the brilliant and later famous scientist Jacob Bronowski accompanied by Mary Eirlys Roberts and the recently married Mary Burtonwood and George Ellidge.

Mary Ellidge became Graves' typist-secretary, fell in love with him and probably had an affair although Miranda Seymour thinks the relationship was limited to kissing.[132] Among the small group of artistically-inclined foreigners, however, it was common for couples to uncouple and couple with others; it would be strange if Graves remained the exception. The Ellidges would leave in separate directions. Cameron became a disciple of Laura, thought her for a time as 'God', may have slept with her, then fled the island and married Elfrieda Faust.

Laura kept criticizing Graves' writing and eventually him for his lack of manliness. While Graves never objected to her demands and insisted that she was perfect and worthy of worship, his diaries show his growing resentment and scepticism. Many of his friends thought her ugly, vulgar and awful, but there were always a few who stayed on, regarded her as brilliant and were willing to accept the situation. From late 1933 onwards it seems that Graves and Laura were getting on each other's nerves, mocking each other, and no longer in love. The pattern was similar to the way his marriage with Nancy frayed. He even found amusement in, and wrote to others about, Laura's chamber pot splitting in half leaving permanent marks on her bottom.[133] By mid-summer 1934 Bronowski, Roberts and the Ellidges were rebelling against Laura's rule and soon left or were sent away. Honor Wyatt and Gordon Glover, both journalists living in Deià, were then invited into the charmed circle.

When Graves needed another typist to replace Mary, Karl Goldschmidt was brought to his attention. Goldschmidt would remain his secretary, assistant, editor and friend over the ensuing decades. A German Jew whose parents had both died when he was young, Goldschmidt came to Majorca on impulse, and knew he could not return to Nazi Germany. He was living in Lluch Alcari, a neighbouring village, needed work, and became a fixture of the Graves establishment. He began to learn English and within a few months was offered a yearly salary to type for both of them; soon he was living in one of their houses, C'an Torrent. He became important to their work, typing, checking facts, researching for books and preparing manuscripts; they would prevent his being forced to return to Germany and arranged for his passage to England where he eventually became a British citizen. He in turn worshipped them.

During the decade Graves first lived in Deià, he was continually swindled by Gelat into spending money on more land and roads that he could not legally own. Gelat realized that by playing up to Laura he could get him to invest in land that he or his family owned. As a result Graves would lose a lot of money on real estate schemes including building a road to the small rocky beach and buying land around it which Laura wanted for a hotel for tourists. After the road was destroyed in a storm Graves became so desperate for money that he wrote to Sassoon for the first time in three years asking for £1,000. This led to an acrimonious exchange of letters during 1933 in which Graves in effect asserted that he had always been right and Sassoon always wrong; Laura was 'the most accurate writer there is'.[134]

Laura agreed. She also thought she could turn the imagined hotel into an international university and had everyone, including Graves, reading about the education systems of the world. A lot of money was wasted on this foolish scheme especially as after the road washed away the attempt to rebuild it on a larger scale led to the Spanish government's becoming concerned with what these foreigners were doing. Graves seemed to take everyone at their professed face value and find no fault in their obvious deceits. He complained in *Good-bye to All That* that his family's intense morality did not prepare him for the cunning and evil of the real world.

Seizin Press

Towards the end of *Good-bye to All That* Graves mentions learning how to print books. This was a time of many small presses, such as the famous Hogarth Press; Virginia and Leonard Woolf had published several of his volumes of poems and three essays in literary criticism. Hogarth Press also published Laura's first book of poems, *The Close Chaplet* (1926), and her *Voltaire* (1927). The former sold 27 copies, the latter 125. In 1930 Nancy Cunard's Hours Press in Paris would publish her *Four Unposted Letters to Catherine* and *Twenty Poems Less* (1930). The small presses were important to the modern movement as writers turned from the public to patrons and a small elite readership for their support. Graves was not a modernist poet, although Laura was, but he was attracted towards having his own publishing imprint for himself and friends. He continued to write poetry every year but publishers did not want slim volumes. In London Graves and Laura had started the Seizin Press and brought the press to Deià. This was important to Laura as trade publishers usually rejected her manuscripts except when Graves made their acceptance a condition of contracting his own writings. Indeed, Graves did not publish in literary journals and other periodicals between 1927 and 1940 because their editors would not accept Laura's work.[135]

Seizin Press publications included Laura's volume of poems *Love as Love, Death as Death* (1928) and *Epilogue*, a hard-cover annual literary magazine she edited which lasted three issues 1935–8, with Graves as Assistant then Associate

Editor. Contributions were mostly the Graves-Riding circle: Reeves, Wyatt, Lye, Matthews, Aldridge, Cameron, Bronowski and Alan Hodge. The fourth issue was edited by Laura as a separate publication. While Graves wrote a few short essays on literary topics, *Epilogue* was not a literary journal. Its wide range was in keeping with Laura's ambitions; the original title was *The Critical Vulgate*.

Although Seizin Press is prominent in the Graves-Riding legend, its publications attracted few buyers and rather than supporting the couple and freeing them, Graves depended on publishers in England and the USA. From 1935, after the success of his Claudius novels, Graves was subsidizing Laura's writings by having Constable in England distribute Seizin Press publications.

Poetry

Graves did publish his own powerful *Poems 1929* and *To Whom Else?* (1931) with the Seizin Press. They praise Laura and show disillusionment with the life he led. There is a new insistence on living in the present without thought and without being deceived. *Poems 1929* includes 'Sick Love' in which the woman is told 'Take your delight in momentariness'.[136] 'In Broken Images' contrasts his failed beliefs and commitments of the past with his present dedication to the senses and his 'new understanding of my confusion'.[137] 'Warning to Children' claims life is an unsolvable puzzle consisting of endless attractions and imaginings each of which leads to further unfulfilled desires and expectations. It is like a box which has within it another box and within that still another box and within that still another. The intricate phrasing of the poem, slightly varying yet repeating itself and leading onward to more of the same, illustrates the continuing expectations and the lack of satisfaction. The opening line of 'Dismissal' sums up his angry realism: 'If you want life, there's no life here.' [138] 'Wm. Brazier' mocks the reader's desire for pastoral nostalgia and romantic sentiments by contrasting false prettiness with reality. It concludes with an attack on readers as fools. Wm. Brazier is a chimney sweep who in the artificial language of poetry 'jingled around town in a pony-trap':

> He would crack his whip at us and smile and bellow,
> 'Hello, my dears!' [If he were drunk, but otherwise:
> 'Scum off, you damned young milliners' bastards, you!']
> Let them copy it out on a pink page of their albums,
>
> Carefully leaving out the bracketed lines.
> It's an old story -f's for s's-
> But good enough for them, the suckers. [139]

Much of Graves' anger was still towards his father. 'Welsh Incident', based on a remembered train journey with Alfred, was in 1929 titled 'Railway Carriage', and originally had the strange creature give off 'a loud belch', which in later editions was changed to the ironic but less offensive

... 'a very loud respectful noise -
Like groaning to oneself on Sunday morning
In Chapel, close before the second psalm.' [140]

So much for his father's conversation! The 1931 volume is dedicated to Laura and her claim that she is the end of 'history' and his goodbye to his past. The title poem concludes

With great astonishment
Thankfully I consent
To my estrangement
From me in you. [141]

There is a mythology in these poems based on Laura's fantasies about herself which Graves encouraged. She claimed magical powers, that she was infallible, that she was divine and even that she was 'finality' – which she associated with the Apocalypse. She had immense notions of grandeur and rapidly went from Gertrude Stein worship to claiming that Stein was the Old Law preparing for Laura. Stein claimed that her experiments with syntax were saving the sentence, so Laura had to up the stakes by claiming to be saving the word. As she had Stein's trick of making the obvious obscure it is at times difficult to know precisely what she meant but her delusions included claims to have replaced the coming of Christ. She understood that Graves wanted her to make such claims and wanted to believe them; she thought such worship of women by men was a way men used women to create art and earn fame.

While her aim to lead an avant-garde revolution of the word and philosophy was absurd, there was a profound feminist insight into how love and even male masochism could be used to dominate women.

At her best Laura wrote witty, difficult, baffling, at times obscure verse, with self-conscious linguistic play, paradox and implied profundities. Although she began by using traditional metrics she did not have a good ear for rhythm or the harmonies of poetry and soon moved on to free verse. Her writing can resemble that of Stein; she is a realist who makes supposedly straightforward thoughts about reality absurdly complicated. She, however, had a sense of humour, can be amusing, even maliciously funny, and always thought of poems as challenging accepted truths. Although the narrative of her verse often consisted of self-pitying allegories, she had the modernist poise of belonging to an intellectual and artistic elite.

Graves was instinctively a popular poet working out of the ballad tradition, mixing simple speech with at times dated poetic diction. He had an excellent feeling for the harmonies of English poetry, a sense of music, rhythm and rhyme. He had studied the art and technique of poetry and would revise through many drafts. Once Laura brought her critical eye to his work, making him justify what he had written, there was an improvement in his poetry. It was cleaner, had backbone, thought. There is an assertiveness which begins in his Laura-period poems, an assertiveness which he learned from her. He also revealed, as the poem 'Wm. Brazier' shows, an immense anger, a desire to curse and defy. Graves remained hurt by the world. He pretended to ignore it, but much of his life seems determined by a desire to have others accept him on his own terms and he raged when they did not.

In *Poems 1926–30* and *Poems 1930–1933* he brought together the main poems of this period. Those of the second volume shout sexual desires and fantasies, but, while showing that he was more realistic, honest and experienced than in the past, the poems continue some of his earlier puritanism and disgust.

> To the much tossed Ulysses, never done
> With Women whether gowned as wife or whore.
> Penelope and Circe seemed as one:
> She like a whore made his lewd fancies run,
>   And wifely she a hero to him bore. [142]

Sex temporarily gives pleasure but afterwards there are 'those same terrors wherewith flesh was racked'. If life is a deceiving sexual odyssey, 'Ulysses' 'loathed the fraud, yet would not bed alone'. [143]

The witty 'Down, Wanton, Down!', the next poem after 'Ulysses', is also about being driven by desire and lack of discrimination in sexual appetite:

> Down, wanton, Down! Have you no shame
> That at the whisper of Love's name,
> Or Beauty's, presto!, up you rise
> Your angry head and stand at gaze?

The penis is a blind soldier compelled to act

Indifferent what you storm or why,
So be that in the breach you die! [144]

'The Succubus' tells of an 'ecstasy of nightmare' with a 'devil-woman' who has a 'paunched and uddered carcasse, fathering brats on you of her own race', but 'is the fancy grosser than your lusts were gross?' [145] Such poems show how Freud's influence led to a sexual openness previously unthinkable. Even the mentions of homoeroticism in *Good-bye to All That* belong to the rejection of Victorian prudery.

After four or five years in Majorca the relationship between Graves and Laura changed. She treated him as a slave and mocked his need to act the domesticated female. She liked dominant men such as Gelat and needed other admirers. Several males fled from the island when Laura suggested that friendship was not enough. From 1934 onwards, as Graves fell out of love with her, his poetry once more began to lose its power although he remained loyal to her and for some years further their lives and literary careers remained entwined.

Novels

The need to support himself and Laura and her taste for a superior manner of living turned Graves into a highly successful novelist which brought his poetry to public attention again. The period 1933–8 was rich in publications including a foolish rewriting of Dickens – *The Real David Copperfield* (1933) – and four major novels, *I, Claudius* (1934), *Claudius the God* (1935), *Antigua, Penny, Puce* (1936) and *Count Belisarius* (1938). His best-known fiction was thought by him hack work although the public liked them more than his poetry and they remain in print.

His poetry was personal, about his life. His short stories, especially those set in Deià, were based on actual events, although he often invented to improve the story. For novels Graves wrote about the past where there was an existing record that he could research, speculate about, and upon which to build. The one exception is *Antigua, Penny, Puce*, a malicious, witty comedy, his one novel set in recent times. It tells of a struggle by a brother and sister over possession of a rare stamp. Oliver Palfrey, a priggish private tutor and aspiring writer, is continually outwitted by clever Jane, a famous actress and dramatist, who seems able to do and be anything she wants. She possesses qualities that Graves found in Laura and in his sister Rosaleen, an assurance and way with the world that he expected in women: 'Every ordinary man will have forgiven Oliver for pulling Jane's hair in his just rage at her meddlesome and undeniably stupid act of separating a block of Newfoundland five-cents, mint, of a quite early issue – 1897, say – just because it looked tidier to have each stamp in a separate oblong! ... And every ordinary woman will have congratulated Jane on her cleverness in getting a strategical hold over her brother. Every ordinary woman will realize that Oliver's selfish and masterful behaviour called for whatever punishment it was in

Jane's power to administer; and, if she laughingly calls Jane a little beast, she will use the word in a complimentary sense. A little beast is a creature who had a superiority in cunning over a little brute.'[146]

While Graves' poetry usually concerns his love life, his prose fiction is about the competition between members of a family in which women are the driving force. The novel concludes with a lawsuit over ownership of the stamp. The legalities about ownership, in which possession becomes more important than right, are not unlike the problem of why Nancy could not get back her silver and her mother's chairs. Who could prove the precise terms in which they had come into the possession of Robert and Laura and why should any Spanish court consider such matters?

While it is possible to interpret the novel politically in relationship to colonialism (who really should own the stamp of a former colony?) or the fight between Communists and Fascists (Jane calls Oliver a fascist), it is more about how Graves saw the relationship between men and women. Oliver is a former public schoolboy concerned with appearances and what he considers the rules of proper behaviour, although faced by Jane's aggression he will cheat. Jane is the imaginative, artistic, competitive, amoral, dominating woman Graves admired. She will love the reckless man who can outcheat Oliver for the stamp.

The four novels were successful, and *I, Claudius* won the James Tait Black Memorial Prize and the Hawthornden; Alexander Korda bought the film rights. Laura, who loathed

Graves' successes, did not like the novel. With the money from the Claudius novels he could send money to Nancy for the children, hire a cook and gardener for Canelluñ, and buy the Posada, a lovely but ruined old house near the top of the village.

I, Claudius and *Claudius the God*

I, Claudius is one of the major novels of the past century if popularity, sales and continuing interest are considered. Although it is not often taught in university courses and there has been no extended critical commentary, it has epic dimensions in which the distant past is made to feel contemporary without any supposed up-to-date relevance being pushed. The relevance is rather in how the characters behave and in the contrast between the Roman ideal of imposing civilized order on the world and the actual amoral, destructive struggle for power. Although far from an historical or metaphysical allegory the two Claudius novels seem a product of the First World War in the disillusionment with empire and in the nihilistic pointlessness of human behaviour.

Whether in war and conquest or politics, family or love, people seek power and status and betray others. Those who do not are the victims of those who do. As in *Good-bye to All That* there is continual repetition; conquered territories rebel or are liberated and need be reconquered, heirs to the throne are poisoned and replaced by others who will also be poisoned. People are denounced, tried and condemned for crimes of which they are innocent and their accusers are later tried and condemned. The famous literary works of Augustus' Rome are attempts to flatter or products of resentment. To write honestly is to court death. The worst fear and tyranny is felt by the small group close to power, the nobility and those in their entourage, who must keep guessing what the emperor, his wife, and influential courtiers want. The best one can do is act honourably and not expect more than survival. In a later essay Graves claims that 'The one Roman virtue was patriotic courage to the point of self-extinction'.[147]

Covering the period from the death of Julius Caesar through the Emperor Augustus, Tiberius, the insane rule of Caligula, and the unexpected succession of Claudius who will be followed by Nero, the two novels tell the history of the Claudian and Julian families. Although emperors may begin by intending to return Rome to republicanism the practicalities of governing soon create tyrants. A grand empire can no longer be governed without a strong central authority and unlimited power. In such scepticism of democracy it is possible to see Graves' own disillusionment with the world and political action. In the history of Rome he found proof that amoral, deceiving authoritarian women made the best rulers. Augustus ruled the world but Augustus was ruled by Livia who married him from ambition not love.[148] Despite the many people Livia poisoned to further her ambitions and authority she was an able and just ruler, unlike the men who were more governed by deceptions, passions, resentments and fears.[149]

I, Claudius is supposedly the autobiography of Tiberius

Claudius Drusus Nero Germanicus (10 BC–AD 54) while living under the emperors Augustus, Tiberius and Caligula. Claudius stammers, is deformed and thought a fool, but he is intelligent and by devoting himself to reading becomes a brilliant scholar who gains a knowledge of people, their ways and useful battle tactics. He also is fated to become emperor through a Sibylline oracle which predicts that 1,900 years later Claudius' autobiography (which he has written in Greek) will be discovered and translated, an amusing allusion to Graves' novel. The novel ends when after the murder of Caligula the terrifying German troops unexpectedly declare Claudius emperor and none of the plotters have the backing to challenge them. The story seems contemporary – with Rome not unlike modern Western empires in the contrast between a proclaimed civilizing mission and the racism of the occupiers:

> The disaster had been due to his imprudence in trying to force civilization on the barbarians too rapidly. The Germans conquered by my father had been gradually adapting themselves to Roman ways, learning the use of coinage, holding regular markets, building and furnishing houses in civilized style, and even meeting in assemblies that did not end, as their former assemblies had always ended, in armed battles. They were allies in name ... But Varus ... began treating them not as allies but as a subject race.[150]

Graves had many Indian friends throughout his life; when writing passages such as the above he would have been conscious of its relevance to the movement to make the British quit India. Quiet contrasts are common to Graves' fiction. The main Roman virtue is supposedly honour, but the actions of the emperors, courtiers, Senate, and military commanders are mostly dishonourable.

Although *Claudius the God* concerns Claudius' reign until he is murdered by Agrippina, the mother of Nero, it begins with a long digression about Herod Agrippa, Claudius' best friend, a secular Jew, partly of Arabian stock, who was raised as a Roman. The stories of Herod and Claudius twine in and out as Claudius proves his worth as a warrior and conquers Britain while his friend has a picaresque life fleeing from debts and conning protectors until he emerges as a mighty ruler in the East who intends to lead the Jews in revolt against Roman rule. His story, while showing the context in which Christianity developed, also mirrors the desire of Roman rulers for deification, even the necessity of providing the ruled with imperial gods they can worship, a need catered to by Claudius being made a god while still alive. As the autobiography does not allow the story to continue after Claudius' death, Graves ends by reprinting three sources for events leading up to his death and subsequent events.

While the two novels offer an account of one of the great moments of history, they are an epic of continuing horror as Claudius evolves from a victim with a strong sense of moral honour to someone larger-than-life who through circumstances and his own disillusionments, especially his marriage to Messalina, becomes as bad as previous rulers.

Ironic contrasts are significant to how we read the novel. Claudius keeps claiming achievements as a result of his intelligence and scholarship, but the reader is aware that Rome and the empire remain corruptly governed.

Graves was a good storyteller who packed his fiction with interesting historical details and clever insights and there was often an autobiographical subtext. The Roman emperors are surrounded by cunning, dominant women, as Graves had been throughout much of his life, and as he especially was now with Laura. Just as Augustus is ruled by Livia to whom he eventually turns over his authority, so Claudius is deceived by Messalina to whom through love he has given his power and who rules corruptly while having other lovers. Claudius is passive and unheroic, while the women are adulterous scheming villains. The plots are tangled but driven by cruelty, conspiracies, and the desire for grandeur. Claudius pretends he does not know the ways of the world and awaits his turn, which may have been how Graves regarded his own situation. The many parallels to Graves in the novel are obvious, even the emperor's stutter. Livia has similarities to Laura. Augustus is impotent with Livia who finds him other women. Livia decides who will marry whom (a trait of Laura who also wanted to keep others under her control). One of the themes of the two novels is the deification of emperors and especially Livia's obsession with being made into a god. The parallel is to Graves' deification of Laura and her self-deification.

Relations between Graves and Laura were further affected by his commercial success with *I, Claudius* and her failure. He was making money and in demand while she could only be published with his support. She claimed that it was disgusting to write historical novels but when she tried it in *A Trojan Ending* it was a disaster.[151] Her novel *14(A)* had bad reviews and was withdrawn when Norah McGuinness, Geoffrey Phibbs' wife, sued for libel. A friend pointed out to Norah that a character based on her was a thief.[152] The novel was an auto-biographical fantasy in which Laura ruthlessly reinterprets the recent past in her own favour and all the other characters are weak, hopeless, and dishonest.

Graves decided to make up with his mother and wrote that he was no longer sleeping with Laura. When Amy visited in 1934, along with his brother John, she realized that Laura had been good for him, providing him with the intellectual and literary company he needed.[153]

Exiled

When Graves and Laura left England in 1929 he imagined returning to a primitive innocence in the mountains of Majorca and that they could ignore the problems of Europe. They were so intent on their personal world of poetry, Laura's redefinition of everything and their circle of acquaintances, that they were surprised in 1936 when the Fascists entered Deià and started killing their opponents. Gelat, the mayor and a socialist, escaped death but was imprisoned. The British consul warned them that they had a choice between taking the last boat leaving Palma or staying behind under Fascist rule.

They fled, leaving everything including their dog Solomon and cat Alice. They were already fed up with the harshness of life in Deià and with each other, although once in exile and homeless they longed to return.

They left Majorca on 2 August 1936 and managed to take Karl Goldschmidt with them on the British ship instead of his being sent on a German ship to likely imprisonment and death. Once in Marseilles the British consul was unhelpful but they travelled by train to Paris, where Graves obtained a visa for Laura; they took the boat-train from Dieppe to England. A friend of a friend made a large house with maids in London available to them. Robert sold some T E Lawrence manuscripts for £1,000 to pay for expenses and immediately began seeing publishers.[154] Soon old friends, Norman Cameron, Alan Hodge, John Aldridge, Lucie Brown and Len Lye and his wife renewed their connection. Laura found an admirer and collaborator in the handsome young poet Hal Kemp. In July 1937 they shared an unattractive house in Ewhurst, a village about 35 miles southwest of London, with Kemp and his wife. Goldschmidt was attracted to and soon married Marie the housekeeper.[155] A few months later, bored with country life, they moved into a large house in London, 31 Alma Square. Alexander Korda, still planning to make a film of *I, Claudius* with Charles Laughton, wined and dined Graves.[156] The actual filming began with Charles Laughton, Merle Oberon, Emlyn Williams and Flora Robson, but Josef von Sternberg who was directing disliked Laughton's acting and when Oberon was injured in a car accident that became an excuse to stop filming.

Laura claimed that her followers of 'The Covenant of Literal Morality', also known as 'The First Protocol' would stop the coming war. This mostly meant writing letters to each other agreeing with her.

Graves made contact once more with his children. Jenny, who from the age of 14 had been a professional dancer, was excited by his movie contacts, especially after Alexander Korda promised to put her into a film. Unfortunately for someone seeking employment in musicals she could not sing and was thought tone deaf.[157]

The run of successful publications in 1938 continued with *Count Belisarius, T E Lawrence To His Biographer Robert Graves*, and *Collected Poems. Count Belisarius* is another cynical story about the ways of the world. Those who are successful and honest cause resentment. It recounts the history of a famous victorious warrior who despite his loyalty was ruined by an emperor who feared that such fame and wealth would result in his being deposed.

Set in the 6th century AD, the novel takes place in the Byzantine or Eastern Roman Empire, after the fall of Rome and the division of Christianity between two Popes, each offering a different doctrine of the nature of Christ, a cause for endless controversies and social disruptions. The Emperor Justinian is a religious fanatic who changes from harassing those he considers heretics to promulgating his own heresies. He hates the best commander of his soldiers, Belisarius, of whom he is jealous and whom he wrongly suspects of planning to usurp him. The more successful Belisarius is the more Justinian finds ways to humiliate him. Justinian claims God will protect his no longer defended empire which is soon conquered by others.

Besides the contrast between Justinian and Belisarius there is Theodora, the emperor's wife, and Antonia, wife of Belisarius, who have the common sense, knowledge of mankind and cunning the two men lack. The views expressed by Eugenius, the narrator, are similar to those Graves held about the natural ability of women to rule and the bad influence of Christianity on society:

> it had been a very long time since a really capable woman had been in so powerful a position as Theodora was. That was the fault of the Church, which – having originated in the East, where women are little better than playthings or slaves or beasts of burden – tended to seclude woman from public life and give them no education worth the name. In pagan times the Empress had often been a second ruler of the state and had acted as a powerful check on the caprices of the Emperor.[158]

The two women have made their way to the top of society after being prostitutes; they understand men and the ways of the world.

Many of the other characters also have remarkable changes in fortune. The narrator, for example, is a captured son of a nobleman; he is sold as a slave, castrated, and after several owners is inherited by Antonia from her mother. Like

Claudius he often implies more than he actually says and is quietly sarcastic and ironic.

The novel has the epic feel of Graves' previous two Roman novels in its scope, with scene changes ranging from Spain to Persia, an immense cast of characters, exciting battles, scandals, great detail, historical interest and larger-than-life characters; the narrative moves rapidly. It would have made a good Hollywood film. Just as the earlier two novels move back and forth between the various troubled areas of the empire and the society and politics of Rome, so *Count Belisarius* shows how the inner strength and failure of the Eastern Roman Empire is determined by the behaviour, especially the fears, jealousies and obsessions, of the emperor and others in Constantinople. Life is like a family struggle in its competitiveness and resentments.

While Belisarius' acceptance of his execrable treatment by Emperor Justinian can be explained by the early oaths he made to his mother (recalling Graves' own upbringing), the conclusion of the novel implies Christ-like behaviour similar to Jesus 'before Pontius Pilate'.[159] The novel has been much praised for its treatment of battles.[160] Taken together, the Claudius novels and *Count Belisarius* illustrate that power corrupts and brings out the worst in individuals, tempting them with their wildest sexual fantasies.

Before T E Lawrence's death in 1935 Graves prepared an obituary with his help; he had a foreboding he would die, and thought that Graves would write what he wanted. The obituary was often republished which led to *T E Lawrence To*

His Biographer Robert Graves (1938), half of a two-volume life published by Faber in England and Doubleday in New York which Graves shared with Basil Liddell Hart.[161] Liddell Hart, a well-off political journalist, introduced Graves to the famous literary agent A P Watt, who would from now on handle his writings. The Lawrence project barely survived Laura's attempt to split Graves from Liddell Hart with whom since 1935 he had a pleasant exchange of letters, each sharing rather contrasting inside information given them by Lawrence.

When Liddell Hart invited Graves and Laura to dinner at his house in London he was shocked by their attacking his writings and ethics, an attack led by Laura, which was followed by a letter of the same nature. When he replied, thinking it expected of him, Graves insultingly claimed that Liddell Hart did not understand the difference in the kinds of criticism being made, 'So communications between us are cut'.[162] Eventually they made up but at the price of Liddell Hart understanding that Laura was always right and he had to become one of those who endorsed her Covenant of Literal Morality and absurd *First Protocol*. Although Graves had brought together a *Collected Poems* in 1927, the 1938 *Collected Poems* published by Cassell was his first careful selection. The problems Laura had in being published are reflected in his many changes of publishers. When Jonathan Cape and Laura fell out, Graves published his Claudius novels with Arthur Barker, who suffered through four of her books before realizing that her future grandiose projects required ending the relationship. Graves then began subsidizing Constable to distribute her

Seizin Press publications including *A Trojan Ending* (1937). In 1938 he began publishing with Cassell which agreed to publish Laura's *Lives of Wives* (1939) along with his *Count Belisarius* novel. Cassell would remain his main British publisher; his *Collected Poems* were paralleled by Cassell also printing Laura's *Collected Poems* the same year.

Laura's new man

England was only a waystation, as it meant high living costs and paying British taxes. Despite the events in Europe, Graves and Laura belonged to the generation of writers and artists who lived abroad. After some months in Switzerland, in 1938 they temporarily settled in France where they shared a house with Beryl Pritchard and Alan Hodge. Laura, however, wanted to return to the USA. In 1939 Tom Matthews, Graves' friend from his Oxford days, an editor of *Time* magazine, invited them and arranged their stay in a farmhouse in Brownburg, near New Hope, Pennsylvania, with Schuyler Jackson and his wife Kit.

Jackson, a heavy drinker and general failure who dabbled in poetry, was vaguely connected with *Time* magazine through his long friendship with Matthews. In his one *Time* article he had surveyed the year's poetry and favourably reviewed Laura's *Collected Poems* in terms based on her own self-indulgent, self-flattering 'To the Reader'; the review was sent to her in France. A correspondence followed which contributed to her desire to return to the USA where she hoped that through

Jackson and *Time* she would at last be recognized as she deserved.[163]

Jackson and Laura were immediately attracted to each other and within six weeks she and Graves, having decided that Jackson's wife and mother of four children was a witch, caused her to have a breakdown, confess to her witchcraft, and be sent to a mental asylum. It is difficult to understand exactly how this was achieved as those involved would not talk about it afterwards, but there were long periods of silences, stares, whispers, signs, and the discovery of supposed proofs. Such behaviour, while abominable, was not untypical of them. Laura had usually obtained what she wanted by any means, especially by creating hysteria, and she and Graves had practised including and excluding people within their Deià circle. She convinced Graves of her magic powers while he believed in ghosts and evil spirits. They would not be the first nor the last whose rejection of rationality and bourgeois conventions resulted in savage lack of consideration of others rather than the new moral purity they sought.

Graves' sometimes abominable behaviour towards his wives, children and friends might be explained by his shell shock but he was always capable of blocking out others from his feelings just as he could focus his emotions on an individual or a few friends. He could be very much the gentleman, even offer to fight duels over discourteous behaviour, but he would turn ruthlessly amoral for his goddesses.

Having rid herself of the wife, Laura rid herself of Graves and later married Jackson. These events became the basis for two books by other writers – Tom Matthews' *Under the Influence* and Miranda Seymour's novel *The Telling* (American title *Summer of 39*). Laura and Jackson moved to Florida where he grew citrus fruit and helped her with her interminable, unpublishable projects to correct the world for which she felt poetry no longer adequate and instead turned to philosophy. For two decades she would remain mostly quiet until Graves began editing her out of his past.

It is easy to mock Laura Riding. She was an interesting person with a minor talent which she wasted by trying too much. She was driven by ambitions first instilled into her by her father, and also by many insecurities, mental instability and the lack of any ability or means to support herself except through the men she could attract. She and Graves were for a time a perfect fit. His life was a mess and he needed someone, preferably a woman, who would tell him what to do and who had no doubt that she was always right.

He turned Laura into a deity whom he had to serve: she came to believe in what he believed, although she often despised him for his servitude and eventually wanted to escape from her role. In *Epilogue III* (1937) Graves expressed what he emotionally needed. In 'From a Private Correspondence on Reality' he claims she could 'perceive human history with eyes trained on it from some point outside. I am aware that your consciousness is of a final quality ... I have always had a blind but obstinate will to discover a consciousness of this quality ... and a physical intuition that it would be a woman's ... there is nothing fantastic in my conviction that you think finally.' [164]

The essay from which this is quoted consists of pages of Laura's unintelligible gibberish with a couple of paragraphs of Graves praising her. The essay is interesting for his admission that he had a terrible fear of death.

Unfortunately Graves could not persuade many others to see what he saw in her and she thought that Schuyler Jackson and *Time* might. For a while Laura hoped to keep Graves as a breadwinner while she submitted to her new man; she would write to Graves in England asking him to keep her doings quiet from their friends. She assumed she could still control him, but understood that he was attracted to another woman, Beryl Pritchard, against whom she kept warning him.

7

Beryl and the War Years

1939–46

Alan Hodge (1915–79), then a student at Oxford, wrote to Laura Riding concerning *Epilogue*; he came to Deià at Christmas 1935 and soon was part of the Graves-Riding circle and a contributor to the annual. After fleeing Majorca, Graves lived near Hodge and Beryl Pritchard in London. In January 1938 Beryl married Hodge, but by the summer Graves was also in love with her. He became attracted when, in July, she, Hodge, Laura and himself shared Château de la Chevrie outside Rennes in France. After Riding and Graves went to the USA, Hodge and Beryl followed. When Laura announced that she and Schuyler were now a couple, Graves returned to England; Beryl, uncertain what to do, stayed behind. Graves discussed the situation with Hodge who said that he and his wife had an unsatisfying marriage; Beryl then joined Graves in England while Hodge worked for him on his writings.

Hodge, who wrote the first draft, was given credit as co-author of *The Long Weekend: A Social History of Great Britain 1918–1939* (1940). In this amusing, packed, sceptical survey of everything from the abdication of King Edward VIII to the Austrian writer Stephen Zweig, Graves used many of the techniques of *Good-bye to All That* and his imperial novels as the focus moved back and forth from the panoramic to individuals, events and anecdotes in presenting an era; as usual the politicians and other leaders lack vision and honesty. Much of the history could be read as autobiography, including the disillusionment of the returning soldiers after the war, the collapse of belief in Christian certainties and the consequent hedonism and sexual experimentation. We are told that single-sex schools create homosexuality which was tolerated at universities. T E Lawrence writes to Graves that he re-enlisted under various names and tried to avoid the public limelight as ways to avoid women. There is an extraordinary tribute to Laura Riding. 'She was the one poet of the time who spun, like Arachne, from her own vitals without any discoverable philosophical or literary derivations: and the only one who achieved an unshakable synthesis. Unshakable, that is, if the premise of her unique personal authority were granted, and another more startling one – that historical Time had effectively come to an end. She was the only woman who spoke with authority in the name of Woman (as so many men in the name of Man) without either deference to the male tradition or feminist equalitarianism: a perfect original.' Riding's claim that war could be avoided if the '"inner circle"' of influential artists, intellectuals, and their patrons lived by a strict standard of honesty is treated seriously.[165]

With a talent for denying reality, Graves told Basil Liddell Hart (21 November 1939) that despite any contrary appearances he and Laura had not been lovers, that he was happy that she found Schulyer whom he liked, and that Laura approved of his being with Beryl. He still idolized Laura and wrote to Liddell Hart (19 February 1940) that she 'reached (for me) a point of shall we say poetic (i.e. hyper-moral) excellence that nobody has ever attained before'. He blamed Schuyler's prejudice against 'the English aristocratic' for her recent rejection of poetry and the opinions she formerly held.[166]

Hodge helped with the research on *Sergeant Lamb of the Ninth* (1940) and *Proceed, Sergeant Lamb* (1941), linked novels set in America at the time of the War of Independence about an Irish soldier who in the second novel joins the Royal Welch Fusiliers, Graves' own regiment. Graves 'now regarded the American Revolution as the most important single event of modern times'; as in his other novels about empires he was critical of how the conquered were treated.[167]

The greater cheapness of living and labour in Ireland has always rendered her a dangerous commercial rival to England. First of all we were forbidden to export cattle, so our landowners turned their land into sheep-walks, and a flourishing woollen industry was presently begun. This industry, which employed thirty thousand families in Dublin alone, was crushed in my grandfather's day by laws prohibiting the export of Irish wool or cloth, not only to England and the colonies, but to any country whatsoever.[168]

When the Irish began manufacturing linen and hemp instead of wool, 'innumerable restrictions' prevented them from competing with the British and Scots anywhere in the world. The Irish, forced to emigrate because of economic conditions, joined with the Presbyterians who fled previously for religious reasons to become the backbone of the American revolution.[169]

As in *Good-bye to All That* and his imperial novels, Graves wrote detailed analysis of military campaigns and claimed that the best drilled and obedient soldiers are those likely to survive and win battles. Contrasted to the wisdom of those on the spot is the incompetent and corrupt government of the empire where jealousy, private profit, favouritism or sheer ignorance undermine the troops abroad through failure to furnish supplies and reinforcements and by sending bad commanders with foolish plans. The American Congress is no better, as success breeds resentment.

There is another autobiographical dimension. Lamb, who has run away from home after disagreeing with his father, regards the American War of Independence as similar to a young man's need to stand on his own. The more the father provides and helps the more a young adult needs to avoid dependence, "'every grown man has the right to live where and how he pleases, in independence'". The American colonies struggling against England are similar in their relationship to

Graves and his father. It is necessary to force the issue through a quarrel; otherwise 'forfeit all dignity of manhood'.[170]

Beryl

By 1940 Beryl, although still married to Alan, was living with and had a child by Graves. This was another version of the trio in which Graves often found himself. Accepting that the relationship with Laura had ended and that he and Beryl could not return to Pennsylvania, they settled from 1940 to 1946 in Vale House, a large damp 18th-century farmhouse in Galmpton, a village near Brixham Harbour, South Devon.

Beryl (1915–2003) was from a well-off family and much younger than Graves. Like most of his women she could be domineering, quarrelsome, and was often in bed ill, in her case from gynaecological problems. Robert's friends thought that she was not naturally commanding but that she was either imitating Laura or he expected such behaviour from his women. Unlike Laura she had little sense of housekeeping or order and life at Vale House was chaotic.[171] Although she had studied Politics Philosophy and Economics at St Anne's, Oxford, she was not an intellectual like Laura, nor a painter like Nancy, but she brought to Graves a calmness that the previous women lacked. Whereas Laura was concerned with herself, Beryl's concerns were Robert, her children, and, eventually, making their house in Majorca a place for a stream of visitors. For about a decade he loved her. There are many excellent poems written to and about her including the exquisite 'She tells her love while half asleep'.[172]

They had three children, William in 1940, Lucia three years later when Alan gave her a divorce, and Juan the next year. Their fourth child, Tomás, was born in Deià. Beryl was an unmarried mother and her children with Graves were legally bastards. Nancy would not divorce him since to do so she would need to use the name Graves and she insisted that she was Nicholson; she was also annoyed with him, who, admitting he was wrong about the past, asked for a new start on returning to England, thus raising Nancy's hopes, and then decided to marry Beryl. He got around the problem by registering William, and obtaining a ration book, as Graves rather than Hodge. Beryl took the name Beryl Graves although they would not marry until 1950 when Nancy agreed to divorce.

They moved into Vale House in May 1940. As only one room and the kitchen had a fireplace the house was cold in winter. Although it lacked comforts there was a radio, in the back was a garden for vegetables, and despite wartime food shortages it was still possible for them to obtain milk, cream and fish, crabs and lobsters locally. Margaret Russell, the nurse whom Nancy fired in 1921, joined them as housekeeper in August 1941.[173]

During 1940 the war was becoming dangerous and an invasion was expected. Graves, otherwise sceptical of governments and wars, retained a strong sense of duty as a soldier and was proud of his time with the Royal Welch Fusiliers: he assumed that he could train officers or find some useful war work, but was rejected as unfit. As a newcomer in the village with the middle name von Ranke, living with an unmarried woman, he was suspect; a local constable spread rumours until it became known that Graves, rather than being a German spy, had been seriously wounded in the previous war, after which he was treated with respect and addressed as Captain. Although too old for active service he joined the Local Defence Volunteers (later the Home Guard). His former secretary and researcher, Karl Goldschmidt, feared deportation and tried to go to Canada. Although he was Jewish, he had been interned but eventually was allowed to join the Army Pioneer Corps and was briefly stationed in Devon.

Soon visitors started arriving, including such old friends as Norman Cameron, and new ones such as Mrs Mallowan, who wrote crime fiction under the name of Agatha Christie, and her husband, Max Mallowan, an archaeologist with whom Robert would discuss his theories about matriarchal cults in the past. Christie dedicated her novel *Towards Zero* (1944) to Graves; the novel uses two love triangles in which someone who is married is in love with someone else.

When a radio talk Graves had given on the lack of new war poets was published in the *Listener*, it brought a letter from a Welsh writer, Second Lieutenant Alun Lewis (1915–44), objecting to the distortion of one of his poems by taking lines out of context. The correspondence lasted until Lewis' death in Burma which the army said was an accident but might have been suicide. Graves read and offered comments on the manuscript of Lewis' second volume of poetry and, by dedicating that volume and his life as a poet to his single poetic theme of Life and Death, Lewis probably gave Graves a shove towards the White Goddess.[174]

In 1941 Graves also met Joshua Podro, a Polish Jew and Hebrew scholar, who influenced the novel *King Jesus*, *The White Goddess*, and such later works as *The Nazarene Gospels Restored* (1953), *They Hanged my Saintly Billy* (1957) and the historical conjectures of *Jesus in Rome* (1957). *King Jesus* (1946) argues that Jesus' family lineage made him the rightful king of the Jews and that the Christian Bible transforms political history into religious mythology. Told as narrative, the story is based on the principle that behind myths there is historical truth to be uncovered by scholarship, linguistics and insight. Graves also became friendly with Joanna and George Simon; their youngest daughter, Julia, would later become one of his muses.

Graves tried to make up with his children by Nancy. As he now had two families to support, had to pay British taxes, and the war badly affected his earnings as a writer, he tried to reduce payments to Nancy, who objected. Catherine had worked with him in fixing up Vale House but he claimed he could not afford for her to go to university. Jenny Nicholson, now an actress and scriptwriter in London, visited him as did Sam. After Jenny's lodgings in London were bombed, she found work with the BBC in Bath, and eventually joined the WAAF. David, who took a third-class degree in English at Cambridge, applied, at Robert's suggestion, and was accepted for the Royal Welch Fusiliers. He would be killed in action in 1943.

Graves' return to the British literary scene was accompanied by several literary movements interested in his writings. During the late 1930s and 1940s he became influential on such poets as Vernon Watkins, Kathleen Raine and George Barker, who sought inspiration in spirituality, myth, the irrational and surrealism. Dylan Thomas, whose work Graves did not like, was the best known of this romantic Bardic school. Graves was after larger game, a rewriting of the early history and pre-history of the West to make poetry and the irrational central to culture; he would be the Bard of his own mythology.

Publications

Despite wartime paper shortages and consequent difficulties in having books published, Graves continued writing, editing and trying to support his life as poet by a variety of literary projects such as *The Common Asphodel* (1949) which collected his essays on poetry, 1922–49. His publications while living in Devon included *Work in Hand* (1942), a small anthology of verse shared with Alan Hodge and Norman Cameron published by Hogarth Press; *The Reader Over Your Shoulder* (1943) which Hodge co-authored; *The Story of Marie Powell: Wife to Mr Milton* (1943); and most importantly *The Golden Fleece* (1944, American title *Hercules, My Shipmate*). He also started *King Jesus* and *The White Goddess*.

No sooner had he finished *The Long Weekend* than, with Hodge, he began *The Reader Over Your Shoulder*, a guide to good writing which examined samples by a range of people. The book was part of a broader movement that included Laura Riding, such literary critics as I A Richards and William Empson, various studies of Practical Criticism and The Use of English, and even the Oxford philosophers with their analysis of words; the assumption was that careful use of language with precise awareness of the significance of terms would make the world a better place – whether in promoting peace, clearing up mystification in philosophy, or teaching people how to resist misleading advertising.

The Story of Marie Powell: Wife to Mr Milton created even more controversy than Graves' later radical rewritings of Christian and Jewish history. The novel is told from the perspective of Marie Powell, the young royalist whom Milton strangely married and who left him, Graves claims, with the marriage unconsummated, precipitating Milton's pamphlets arguing in favour of divorce. Marie's parents owed Milton money and Graves assumes that she married the poet to pay her father's debts; Milton was so entranced by her long hair as to be willing to be united with a royalist. The novel shows Graves' usual scholarship and wide reading in its details of 17th-century domestic life, sports and festivals. Many critics and readers were unwilling to accept that the great poet could be a bully towards women and criticised Graves for being unable to feel the power of *Paradise Lost* and being unsympathetic to Milton's character and politics. Graves later replied with 'The Ghost of Milton' (1947), a short article, reprinted in *The Crowning Privilege*, offering his sources especially in Jonathan Richardson's *Explanatory Notes on Milton's Paradise Lost* (1734). It is typical of Graves to have good sources supporting his unconventional claims. He goes further in arguing that Milton is not a great poet as he was more concerned with demonstrating his learning and power than in writing about love.

Although he thought reading Milton depressing, he impressively analyzed the harmonies of Milton's *Lycidas* to show that Samuel Johnson was wrong in his well-known claim that the poem was harsh, the rhymes vague, the rhythms awkward. 'The initial consonants of the first lines are an alliterative interlace of Y.M.L. which is interrupted by the harshness of the alliterative pairs B.B., C.C., F.F.... . The interlace of C.S.D. in the next two lines is linked to the foregoing with another B.B.... . Then follows a more complicated interlace: a P.H.N.L. sequence connected to the C.S.D. sequence by a bridge of D's, and followed by a watery succession of W's to close the stanza.'[175] That is literary criticism written by a poet; Graves always looks closely at writing. He suggests that Milton learned such interlacing of consonants from Welsh bards. Because of his reputation as a novelist his *Collected Poems 1938–45* (1945) sold out the original print run of nearly 5,000 copies; it also received excellent reviews and Graves felt he was now recognized as a major poet.

Goddess worship

Graves' seeming lack of any relationship to the internationalist Modernist movement is deceiving; for a time he thought of himself as a modern before rejecting the modern world, published in Modernist publications, early identified Modernist literature and rejected it, but his writing and thought have many of the same influences although he took them in different directions. Although he wrote prose to earn a living from a middle-class readership his notion of a poet was of a lineage in which art for art's sake was transformed into Modernist notions of pure art. His concise lyrics, although of autobiographical origins, have the economy and finish of impersonal objects. Even the mythology which informs much of his later writing has its parallels in the mythologies that W B Yeats and other 20th-century poets invented to ground their work in a spiritual dimension. Similar to such Modernists as T S Eliot he would turn from the present to an idealized or savage past as the basis for cultural revitalization. Like the Modernists he was an elitist who sought spiritual renewal in the primitive. Although he hated D H Lawrence, both of them rejected England by living abroad, both lacked respect for conventional notions of marriage, both were attracted towards strong-willed women, both were obsessively concerned with the sexual, and both writers attempted to plot new relationships between men and women while being suspected of obscuring the homoerotic in their character.

It was at Vale House that Graves, strongly influenced by his years with Laura, started reinventing European history to explain the link between his poetry to his adoring, masochistically submissive relationship to women. It was difficult to accept being rejected by Laura and her submission to another man. He needed to write her out of his personal history and to place her behaviour within an eternally recurring scheme. Variously expressed, this would be the main subject of his writing for the rest of his life, and the source of his poetics and its mythology in *The White Goddess*. As usual he was working on several books at once and it is at times difficult to know where one ends and another begins. He claimed that during 1943 he suddenly understood that much of the world's mythology referred to an earlier dominant culture in which women ruled and worshipped a female deity. He felt that he had 'a key which unlocks a succession of doors in Roman and Greek religion, and (because the Jewish religion was a Semite one engrafted on a Celtic stock) also unlocks the most obstinate door of all – the story of the Nativity and Crucifixion'.[176]

A draft of *The White Goddess* existed by 1944 and many of its main themes were already present in *The Golden Fleece*, especially the earlier book's 'Prologue'. Although Graves would continue to add to *The White Goddess* until its 1948 publication, and add and revise the 1950 and 1961 editions, the central argument is in the historical novel.

The Golden Fleece, a retelling of the voyage of Jason and the Argonauts, like *The Nazarene Gospel Restored* and many other of Graves' writings from now on, imagines European history, mythology and religion as a conflict between an original matriarchy based on goddess worship and a conquering patriarchy headed by a male deity. He claims that originally women dominated society, chose their sexual partners, of whom they had many, especially at ritualistic orgies which were thought necessary for planting crops, and that men were their slaves; the situation reversed when the Greeks conquered the goddess-worshipping Mediterranean societies and forced on them a supreme male god, a concept followed by the Jews and Christians.

This began a fall from an essentially peaceful natural social and spiritual order to our present discontents. Whereas women know to whom they give birth (and the father does not matter) a patriarchal structure, with the need to be assured that children are the product of the father's sperm, enslaves women into marriage and monogamy which leads to adultery, jealousy and war. Just as Graves had no hesitation in inventing while rewriting history for his Claudius novels, so now he would see everything in relation to his White Goddess mythology, treating legend and gospel as factual history which disguises an actual struggle between the Goddess and her enemies.

This mythology with its revisioning of established European history, literature and legend, leads to Graves as the only modern celebrant of the cult. Since all real poetry is written in praise of the Goddess, he is the only true contemporary poet.

While Graves had long believed that the original culture of the West was matriarchal, the curious masochistic form it took was shaped by his years with Laura. The 'Prologue', also called 'Ancaeus at the Orange-Grove', to *The Golden Fleece* is set in ancient Deià where it is claimed that goddess worship long remained pure and unaffected by the Greek male monotheism which was supplanting it elsewhere along the Mediterranean. The portrait and justification of this pure matriarchy makes the novel worth reading.

The argument is set out in the 'Prologue' where the Nymph of the Orange grove in Deià objects when told of the patriarchal ways elsewhere:

The woman, not the man, is always the principal: she is the agent, he the tool always. She gives the orders, he obeys. Is it not the woman who chooses the man, and overcomes him by the sweetness of her perfumed presence, and orders him to lie down in the furrow on his back and there riding upon him, as upon a wild horse tamed at her will, takes her pleasure of him and, when she has done, leaves him lying like a dead man?[177]

While it might be over-clever to find an unconscious allusion in 'riding upon him, as upon a wild horse tamed at her will', the passage not only offers a future programme but defence of the past in which slavish obedience to the female is rewarded sexually. In this role-reversal the man is used rather than 'agent'. He is reduced to a 'tool'.

In seeking a return to a supposed original matriarchy Graves was also offering a political model, as he claims that men by nature will always fight for domination. One reason why women will not limit themselves to one man, the Nymph explains, is that sharing their favours brings peace:

Here my mother and I distribute our favours evenly among all the fraternities. It is not wise to let any fraternity secure the supremacy, nor to let a king reign beyond two or three years at the utmost: men have a great capacity for insolence if they are not kept in their proper place, and fancy themselves to be almost the equals of women. By insolence they destroy themselves and cause vexation to the women into the bargain.[178]

Is it reading too much significance into Graves' prose to suggest that 'supremacy' contains 'sperm'? While Graves' spokeswoman is talking about nations fighting for dominance, the basic model is men fighting over women whom they want to impregnate to bear their children. Thus matrimony is essential to patriarchy but patriarchy will always result in instability as men fight for supremacy.

The Golden Fleece shows how Graves' imagination formed his own version of Western pre-history. Although at times the novel seems a mad retelling of ancient history and pre-history in which assertion and endless lists of questionable facts and background information pile up relentlessly, the story reads well, sustains attention and, as usual, Graves' prose is rapidly paced and clear, even if the diction is careless, a reflection of the speed at which he produced his popular fiction. It is typical of Graves that he should assume the legend of the Golden Fleece referred to actual historical events concerning the transformation of Europe's culture from Goddess to Father worship and that he should assume he could explicate the true events and their significance by using his imagination along with intensive reading of relevant material. The material was so real to him that he made four detailed maps of the voyage of the Argonauts to be published with the book.

The Golden Fleece received excellent reviews and the 9,000 copies rapidly sold out in England; because of the wartime paper shortage it would be a while before it could be reprinted. Despite poor reviews of the badly produced Creative Age Press American edition, it also sold well.[179] It is translated into many languages and continues to be republished. My paperback copy was published by Pyramid Books, New York, along with *Count Belisarius* and *Homer's Daughter* in 1966.

Under the influence of his new vision of the world and the role of the poet as the White Goddess' celebrant Graves had become a major poet. The first signs can be found in *Work in Hand* – 'Language of the Seasons' and more significantly 'Mid-Winter Waking', a love poem to Beryl which could also be interpreted as about his Muse and the White Goddess. It has a new intensity of feeling and language:

> Stirring suddenly from long hibernation,
> I knew myself once more a poet
> Guarded by timeless principalities
> Against the worm of death, this hillside haunting,
> And presently dared open both my eyes.[180]

He claimed to have discovered an ancient culture worshipping a cosmic order that still existed although it became occulted when the Greeks forced on others the worship of a male deity.

While the claims that humankind was originally governed by a sexually free matriarchy which worshipped a goddess until patriarchy imposed a male deity, matrimony and property rights, can be traced to Johann Bachofen and Jane Harrison, another influence on *The White Goddess* was Margaret Murray (1863–1963) who wrote *Witch Cult in Western Europe* (1921). Murray believed that a universal ancient pre-historical religion with its own calendar and rituals of sacrifice and sexual orgies survived in the witch covens revealed during witchcraft trials. Graves similarly claims the theme of goddess worship with its seasonal calendar or thirteen months and accompanying rituals was preserved by the peasantry and considered witchcraft by Christianity. His choice of words clearly alludes to Murray's thesis. The theme 'was also secretly preserved as religious doctrine in the covens of the anti-Christian witchcult'.[181] Murray, a suffragette and trained anthropologist, had also been influenced by the idea of the sacrificial king in Frazer's *The Golden Bough*. If Graves did not identify Murray as an influence it was because her argument had taken a different turn from his. She had her covens of witches worshipping an ancient male deity, who became a horned devil, a very phallic god, a view she argued in more detail in *The God of Witches* (1933, 1952).

By rediscovering and living by the rules of ancient matriarchy Graves became its poet, the only true poet of modern times. This cosmology put his previous life with Nancy and Laura into a meaningful context and gave significance to his relationship with Beryl. It would justify any new loves, as the story was dramatic, with the Goddess tiring of lovers and finding new ones, while the poet must seek her temporary incarnations in women who would be his muse. Everything, all life, became charged with aspects of the Goddess and Graves was her poet. When Juan was born on the Winter Solstice it hardly seemed a coincidence and led to Graves writing one of his best, most intense and most famous poems, 'To Juan at the Winter Solstice':

> There is one story and one story only
> That will prove worth your telling,
> Whether as learned bard or gifted child;
> To it all lines or lesser gauds belong
> That startle with their shining
> Such common stories as they stray into.

The poem continues by alluding to the all-encompassing original pre-Greek mythology that Graves would claim he discovered in his research for what was then called 'The Roebuck in the Thicket' and which soon became *The White Goddess*. Each story told by any true poet, including bits of true poetry found in lesser works, is an expression of the Goddess:

> Dwell on her graciousness, dwell on her smiling,
> Do not forget what flowers
> The great boar trampled down in ivy time.
> Her brow was creamy as the crested wave,
> Her sea-grey eyes were wild
> But nothing promised that is not performed.[182]

'The Twelve Days of Christmas' interprets the birth of Jesus as a story about the Goddess and matriarchy being replaced by her son and patriarchy:

> The impassioned child who stole the axe of power,
> Debauched his virgin mother
> And vowed in rage he would be God the Father.[183]

Much of Graves' life and writing is a conflicted version of this struggle to declare himself independent of his domineering mother and a guilty slavery to other women whom he transformed from whatever they were into domineering goddesses.

The White Goddess provided Graves with a set of beliefs and mythology to replace the Christianity he lost during the First World War. Having such a theme allowed him to make his lyrics part of a continuing narrative with resonances ranging from the autobiographical to the divine. It was also his poetic theory. Would the woman, the poem, the Goddess, visit him tonight?

The wild insights and distant associations that came to him while working on the book were a period of inspiration, poetry beyond the act of writing poetry. He was the poet as madman-scholar-genius and in letters he kept asking why no one else ever saw the connections now so obvious to him. He had long been interested in the unconscious and seemingly irrational elements in poetry, and he had mocked academic scholars for their conventionality and lack of insight; suddenly he felt he had a method, the true poet's method, of seeing how to solve seemingly insolvable problems. 'I have had to face such "puzzling questions, though not beyond all conjecture", as Sir Thomas Browne instances in his *HydrioItaphia*: "what song the Sirens sang, or what name Achilles assumed when he hid himself among the women." I have found practical and unevasive answers to these and many other questions of the same sort.' [184] The claim that the true poet uses inspired

associations to make unexpected connections was the basis
of many of his lectures and essays over the coming decades.
To those who demanded proof he would turn the problem
around and ask how the questioner could prove his or her
spiritual beliefs.

Leaving England

As the war was ending Graves began seeking ways to return to
Deià and Canelluñ. He found an aviation company willing to
charter to him a small aeroplane and a pilot who would go to
Majorca by way of stops in France. The pilot had once flown
Franco and had good relations with the Spanish government.[185]
Departure was to be on 15 May 1946 from Croydon Airport.
Before leaving Graves decided not to sign a petition given him
by T S Eliot asking pardon for Ezra Pound, then imprisoned
in the USA for treasonous broadcasting for Fascist Italy during
the war. Graves wrote Eliot that as he did not consider Pound
a poet he could not honestly sign. Graves also re-established
contact with Gertrude Stein, after six years of silence due to a
quarrel Laura had caused by taking exception to Stein's attempt
at good manners. In describing the breakup with Laura he now
(28 January 1946) explained her as one of many women on
whom the White Goddess descended for a time. This was
to become his model for writing about his relationship to
women: 'it's a strange but familiar story. She was possessed for
a great many years by a very cruel and beautiful Muse with
which she identified herself; and then she found the position

intolerable, and the spirit left her and she became common clay, an average American divorcée-remarried housewife, with a repudiation of all her works.' Graves claimed that from 1930 onwards his relationship with Laura was becoming painful.[186] His ego could not stand rejection; instead of Laura choosing someone else she had been deserted by her Muse.

Karl Goldschmidt and his wife Marie were supposed to follow Graves and Beryl to Majorca, but Karl had fallen in love with another woman. Knowing that Graves was also interested in her, Karl put off moving. After being invalided out of the Navy he once more became Graves' typist. When Graves invited him to move into Vale House he accepted and left his wife Marie with her parents in Sussex.[187] At Vale House he met Rene (Irene), an attractive young woman who lived in Brixham, and whose husband, from whom she would soon separate, was away in the military. Once a week, on Fridays, she came to Vale House to cook a meal and both men had their eye on her. She was an influence on Graves' work on the White Goddess.[188] Karl was waiting to be accepted as a British citizen and hoped that he and Rene could divorce their partners and marry.

8

Return to Deià, First Muse

1947–59

The 1940s and 1950s were a great period for Graves' writing which included some of his best poems along with translations of classics and retellings of the Bible, Greek and Hebrew myths as he tried to rewrite the foundations of Western history to fit into the Goddess-worshipping culture that he claimed preceded the Greeks and which was the source of genuine poetry. During these years he was obsessed with a vision and almost every year there was a volume of new poems or a new collected or selected poems reflecting his love life.

The White Goddess (1948) was rejected by many publishers before Faber accepted it after T S Eliot, thinking it strange and wild, recommended it. Until publication Graves kept sending many bits and pieces to be added to the manuscript. The book combines older anthropological notions of an original matriarchy that preceded patriarchy with the exegesis of White Goddess worship in Celtic literatures and asserts that the only true poetry is that devoted to and inspired by such a muse. 'The Dedication' to *The White Goddess*, which would be published in *Poems and Satires* (1951) as 'The White Goddess', alludes to his search for her and how she inhabits women the poet loves. It offers a poetics based on true love being wild and destructive:

> All saints revile her, and all sober men
> Ruled by the God Apollo's golden mean –

She is the goddess of love, inspiration and what might otherwise seem irrational thought and behaviour. Graves makes a sustained analogy between himself and explorers, heroes and the mythological, as he proclaims that he is devoting his life to the Goddess, although he knows she will be cruel, betray him, and her power will flit from woman to woman whom he must pursue:

> ... we are gifted, even in November
> Rawest of seasons, with so huge a sense
> Of her nakedly worn magnificence
> We forget cruelty and past betrayal,
> Heedless of where the next bright bolt may fall.[189]

By studying the ancient literature of Ireland and Europe he claimed rediscovery of the original culture of Europe. 'My thesis is that the language of poetic myth anciently current in the Mediterranean and Northern Europe was a magical language bound up with popular religious ceremonies in honour of the Moon-goddess, or Muse, some of them dating from the Old Stone Age, and that this remains the language of true poetry ... The language was tampered with in late Minoan times when invaders from Central Asia began to substitute patrilinear for matrilinear institutions and remodel or falsify the myths to justify the social changes. Then came the early Greek philosophers who were strongly opposed to magical poetry as threatening their new religion of logic, and under their influence a rational poetic language (now called The Classical) was elaborated in honour of their patron Apollo and imposed upon the world.' [190]

The White Goddess is the underlying mythology of the poems of the last decades of his life. It brings together various themes found scattered in his writings and should be understood as his Credo. The mélange of sources, assumptions, good and bad scholarship, claims of secret languages and other oddities, has given the book a bad name with academics but it has proved popular with feminists, Wiccas, neo-pagans, New Age spiritualists and many poets. It offered a renewed romanticism at a time when the major poets were ironic, rational, skeptical and conservative. While Graves was asserting that the only true poetry was that in which the writer and his craft were devoted to the muse Goddess, he was also extending his romantic view that poetry derives from areas of the mind beyond reason and rationality. Many do not finish *The White Goddess*, but it is essential for understanding obscure allusions in Graves' poetry and provides a context for his later works, including reinterpretations of classical and biblical history.

It was followed by *Seven Days in New Crete* (1949), an amusing, ironic novel which imagines a society dominated by goddess worship. This was influenced by Samuel Butler's *Erewhon*. Another, less successful, novel inspired by Butler was *Homer's Daughter* (1955) which assumes that *The Odyssey* was written by Homer's daughter Nausicaa, an idea suggested by Butler in a lecture. Miranda Seymour notes that *Homer's Daughter* offers an unhappy view of marriage with a shrewish wife who has a physically attractive husband who might be taken for Robert Graves, a sign that he was already bored with Beryl.[191]

Greek myths

Graves' many books about Greek and Hebrew myths and Greek, Jewish and Christian history – such as *The Nazarene Gospel Restored* (1953) and *Jesus in Rome* (1957), both of which had Joshua Podro's aid, and the exegetical retelling of *The Greek Myths* (1955), published in two volumes by Penguin – rewrite the basis of Western history and culture. It was an absurd but fruitful enterprise which, while fulfilling his own psychological needs, earned money and brought controversy and fame.

The Greek Myths is itself an epic in which Graves arranged the many legends, plays, stories and fragments of ancient Greece into a continuous narrative beginning with creation myths to the fall of Troy and return home of Odysseus. Much of the material was not properly what he considered 'true myth'. True myth may be defined as the reduction to narrative shorthand of ritual mime performed on public festivals, and in many cases recorded pictorially on temple walls, vases, seals. Such records of true mythologies were unlike philosophical allegories, satires, romances, political propaganda, comic plays and heroic tales, although in practice Graves made use of them as well in his book. He offered a method: 'When making prose sense of a mythological or pseudo-mythological narrative, one should always pay careful attention to the names, tribal origin, and fates of the characters concerned; and then restore it to the form of dramatic ritual, whereupon its incidental elements will sometimes suggest an analogy with another myth which has been given a wholly different anecdotal twist, and shed light on both.' [192]

The narrative brings together all of Greek drama and several epics as well as many other sources, turning them into a linked story. Graves' ability to epitomize, précis and join as well as his encyclopaedic range is remarkable, showing skills he developed in his novels. He is not just making a new story from many old ones, he is offering an authoritative dictionary of Greek culture and its sources. *The Greek Myths* can be read like fiction, but it is also meant for looking up people, legends and allusions, and their various sources.

As such it is a major work of scholarship. There are 171

sections including the five ages of man, the castration of Uranus, the Fates, the birth of Eros, the gods of the underworld, the Oracles, Leda, Endymion, Sisyphus, Mida, Narcissus, Oedipus, Tantalus, the birth of Hercules, the Argonauts, Medea, Paris and Helen, and the Wooden Horse of Troy.

Each of the 171 topics is numbered and subdivided into numbered subsections offering alternative versions of the story. After each topic there are concise references to the many sources Graves used including those for the alternative versions. The narrative and sources would in themselves be a remarkable attempt at synthesis, but Graves, after telling the story and giving its sources, offers exegesis of what is likely to be the basis of the story. The analysis is cross-referenced to related or further versions. Such analysis might be correct but much of it seems like guessing. What, for example, is behind the story of the Trojan Horse? One suggestion is that the Greeks used siege towers covered with horsehide.

Behind analysis of details is another linked story, the story found in *The White Goddess* and *The Golden Fleece* of a prehistoric matriarchal goddess-worshipping culture challenged by an invading patriarchal culture which at first is given a secondary role and eventually usurps and transforms society and starts history as we know it. In his 'Introduction' Graves claims: 'The whole of Neolithic Europe, to judge from surviving artifacts and myths, had a remarkably homogeneous system of religious ideas, based on worship of the many-titled Mother-goddess, who was also known in Syria and Libya.' There were no male gods, only the all-powerful Great Goddess who 'took lovers, but for pleasure, not to provide her children with a father'. Men feared, adored, and obeyed the matriarch whose shrines celebrated childbirth. Graves explains that the moon's three phases, new, full, and old, corresponded to the seasons and the three stages of a woman's life: maiden, nubile, crone. Only after it was recognized that sexual intercourse was needed for procreation did the status of men improve, first with women choosing lovers who were sacrificed annually as symbols of fertility. As in *The White Goddess* details of cultural and historical events accumulate, being supported with discussion of Southern Indian and West African practices, as if the past were known and everything fits seamlessly together, although Graves admits that what he has written is conjectural.[193]

The interpretations and details offered make his view of history appear established fact, although there is often little or no surviving evidence, and Graves needs to go behind and beyond the topic under discussion to show the relevance he assumes. Under the 'Five Ages of Man': 'Hesiod was a small farmer, and the hard life he lived made him morose and pessimistic. The myth of the silver race also records matriarchal conditions – such as those surviving in Classical times among the Picts, the Moesynoechians of the Black Sea (*see 151.e*), and some tribes in the Baleares, Galicia, and the Gulf of Sirté – under which men were still the despised sex, though agriculture had been introduced and wars were infrequent. Silver is the metal of the Moon-goddess.'[194] By arranging the Greek myths into a chronological sequence Graves was once more writing a version of his thesis that all worthwhile stories are essentially aspects of the one story worth telling. He would later similarly treat the Hebrew Myths.

The Greek Myths was highly successful; it rapidly sold out and was reprinted the same year and reprinted with 'amendments' two years later, in 1957. A revised edition was published in 1960 and reprinted regularly every year or two. There were offshoots such as a short *Illustrated Edition* (1981), condensed by John Buchan-Brown, published without the scholarly or interpretative apparatus, which has been regularly reprinted.

The various books about Christianity were controversial and taken together as an argument seemed to jump from here to there, although they represented a sequence as Graves discovered the White Goddess behind everything. He said (in *King Jesus*), as he worked out his conflicting ideas, that Jesus was an heir of David and rightfully claimed the Jewish throne, and (in *Jesus in Rome*) that Jesus married Mary Magdalene, survived the crucifixion, realized that he was not the Messiah and that he had misled his followers, and that he lived afterwards in Rome and later wandered eastward to Kashmir where he was buried in Srinagar. Few of these claims were original (I and other tourists to Srinagar have been shown Jesus' tomb). In another version Jesus, like many other male deities, was really a son of the White Goddess whom she allowed to appear to usurp her divine powers although she kept them for future use. Everywhere Graves looked he saw survivals of the White Goddess: even the drug culture of the 1950s and 1960s attempted to return to earlier shamanism in which frenzied, drugged initiates had orgies worshipping the goddess.

Return to Deià

During May 1946 Graves, Beryl and their three children flew in a private chartered aeroplane to France, first to Rennes, then to Toulouse continuing on to Barcelona and on 18 May reached Palma de Majorca, the first civilians to arrive by air since before the war. Gelat drove them to Deià and soon Robert was back in Canelluñ where he had lived with Laura and written his Claudius novels. Almost everything was still in place, but there were food shortages and the village could no longer celebrate its pagan festivals. Only one expatriate, an English spinster painter, had stayed on throughout the war.

Republican Spain with its civil marriages and Socialists and Communists had been replaced by Fascist Spain ruled brutally by the Falange which, seeking political and religious unity, enforced a reactionary Roman Catholicism. There was an obsession with national purity in ideology and race. Civil marriages were no longer recognized, and the enemy consisted of Republicans, democracy, the enlightenment, Jews, Masons, Protestants, anything foreign, and anything regional such as writing in Catalan. Those who were on the Republican side during the Civil War were either murdered or barred from any dignified employment. Those in the professions, such as lawyers and teachers, were suspect, and if they escaped death would spend decades finding employment only as cleaners. In Deià many Republicans were killed by being thrown from high cliffs.

Deià was an odd place for an Englishman with exotic beliefs to bring his unmarried mistress and their three unbaptized children. To Robert it was the home from which he had been made to flee a decade ago, and also, perhaps as important, a way to avoid British taxes on his earnings as a writer; he would no longer be resident in England for tax purposes provided he kept away most of the year. He was happy to be back in Deià but the place, culture and language were alien to Beryl and the children who had to cope with two new languages, Spanish and the Majorcan version of Catalan, while continuing to speak English at home. Graves had not come to Majorca to become Spanish; he was in the tradition of Englishmen who lived abroad in countries, especially along the Mediterranean, where life was cheaper and servants still affordable, paid little tax, and remained British. He subscribed to an airmail edition of the *Times* and the family listened to the BBC on the radio. His children would be expected to attend Spanish schools and yet be educated for Oxford.

Beryl noticed evidence of Laura throughout Canelluñ, including strange symbols on the walls. At Laura's request, Graves got rid of her old papers, including unfinished books and drafts of poems, some of which he sold to a paper merchant. The centenary of his father's birth was on 22 July, but Graves ignored it although it was publicly celebrated in Ireland and by the family. During October Jenny visited and found that William was already attending the local boys' school while the nuns were helping with Lucia.

The problems of living away from modern facilities became apparent during August 1947 when William was hit by a car when out cycling. It appeared that he would need be sent to surgeons in England; there was, however, an excellent doctor in Barcelona. Robert took him there and stayed until late September when Beryl came for a minor operation she needed and he returned to Deià to supervise Lucia and Juan.[195] William recalled this as one of the few periods he spent much time with his father, who entertained him with songs, stories and jokes; otherwise he was usually distant and busy. Beryl was even more so.

Even in Barcelona Graves could not give up writing and began *Seven Days in New Crete* (1949, American title *Watch the North Wind Rise*), an anti-utopian novel set in an idealistic future where sexual pleasure is not limited to marriage and reproduction, there is no money and even war has been transformed into a game. The novel turns into a thinly disguised autobiography in which Graves re-examined his life with Laura and allowed that while he was happier with the woman Antonia (who represents Beryl), he felt more intensely for Erica (Laura) with her malicious tongue and rapid shifts from being sexually exciting to evil. Venn-Thomas (Graves) admits that Erica treated him badly but he shared her views. Graves would continue to work on the novel after doing proof revisions of *The White Goddess*.[196]

Graves was officially divorced from Nancy on 18 November 1949; six months later, on 11 May, he married Beryl at the British Consulate in Palma with their friends the Camerons as witnesses: the Podros, Karl and Rene were also present. A party followed on a friend's yacht. In the next months there were holidays visiting friends and family in Italy and England, including seeing his mother in Wales. As Amy Graves was suffering from cancer and the ill-effects of X-ray treatment, Robert, Beryl and the three children visited her. Amy was happy for the chance to meet her new grandchildren and to be reconciled with her son. (When she died of brain cancer early in 1951 at the age of 93, Robert did not attend her funeral and at least outwardly seemed unperturbed. The many years of family quarrels about his life had left scars.) At a meeting with T S Eliot about *The Nazarene Gospel Restored* which Graves was working on with Joshua Podro, Eliot was less happy with Graves' biblical scholarship than he was with his research on the White Goddess as a source of poetic inspiration.

Graves was writing well during this period, many of his poems are inventive and have an energetic power. 'Counting the Beats', which written about the December 1949 death from cancer of Julie Matthews, the wife of his friend Tom Matthews, imagines two lovers aware that one is dying. Despite its morbid topic the poem is beautifully lyrical:

Counting the beats
Counting the slow heart beats,
The bleeding to death of time in slow heart beats,
Wakeful they lie.[197]

There was a problem about land along the road to the beach being registered in Juan Gelat's name. In 1949 while he was dying, a heavily drugged Gelat willed the property to his widow and her daughters; Graves had not taken the matter seriously until 1953 when he once more had to buy it, this time from Gelat's widow who claimed her husband earned the land by taking care of Graves' property during the decade he was away.[198]

There were other problems; the easiest to solve should have been the education of the three children which locally was not up to the standards they would need for their futures. William S Merwin, now a famous poet, then a recent Princeton University graduate who had been teaching in Portugal and who was living in Deià with his wife, was hired as the children's tutor. He became a victim of a problem which could never be solved. Graves would become bored with marriage, desire another woman, and need a rival to keep up the excitement of courtship and competition. As a poet he needed a new muse who was regarded as the temporary abode of the White Goddess and whom he had to court, obey, worship, and compete for if he were to be a true poet.

In *The White Goddess* Graves claimed to reveal the hidden original mythology and culture which had ruled most of the world until it was overthrown by patriarchy. His claim, although using eccentric sources and based on often disputed interpretations, had been advanced by earlier generations of cultural anthropologists; except for the fullness of his argument and his exegesis of previously unsuspected sources in ancient literatures, he was in the rearguard of what was still advanced thought during his university years. He, however, made two important additions to the notion that matriarchy was the original culture of the world; he claimed that all true poets celebrate the female deity and further that She incarnated herself in ordinary women for limited periods of time. These incarnations became the temporary embodiment of the goddess as Muse of Poetry. Graves claimed that he could only be a true poet if he devoted himself to writing about and love of such women. Whether regarded cynically as a lecher's charter or more charitably as a needed source of poetic inspiration, and, psychologically, as a way to make sense of his life with Laura, Graves would devote the last decades of his life to his muses.

One theme of such poetry is the lack of sexual excitement in marriage for both the woman and the man. He assumed, or learned, that marriage would eventually leave a wife as disappointed and disappointing as her husband. For all their obsessive chasing a fantasy of ever-passionate love, the later poems continue the quest for honesty and truth that he and Laura claimed to seek and which had been part of his revolt against his parents, school, and 'All That'. In 'With Her Lips Only' conventionality leads to dishonesty. Family life, the raising of children, prevent following the truth of feelings. The 'honest wife' is dishonest in having refused an affair by telling herself she was denying love for the sake of her children, then pretends to love her husband:

Not with her heart but with her lips only;
'For the children's sake', she argues with her conscience,
'For the children' – turning suddenly cold towards them.[199]

The rhymes, musicality, development of the argument as well as the structure of the sonnet form in 'With Her Lips Only' are treated subtly and feel natural.

Judith

Now that his marriage made Beryl a wife Graves became restless, especially after she had an operation removing an ovary which resulted in her regaining her health and taking over many of the domestic chores he habitually did. As she became a good wife she lost the attraction of a mistress and devotion needed for a muse, and, ironically, gave him free time to pursue other women. He unsuccessfully tried to attract several before settling on Judith Bledsoe, a tall 17-year-old American beauty who came to Deià, about whom Graves would write a short story, 'The Whitaker Negroes', in which her name is Julia Fiennes. She had been living in Paris with an artist, and came to Deià hoping that if she met the author of *I, Claudius* it might lead to a film career.

Just as Laura had created a fantasy of leading a small select group of insiders who would save the world, so Graves after *The White Goddess* began to act on the assumption that the mythology he invented was real and that he was the one person who might bring back worship of the Goddess and her culture. Indeed if he were to be a true poet he had to offer devotion to the Goddess as he found her in various women who would be his muses. The first officially was Judith. Graves would write several poems directly about her including 'Darien'.

It is a poet's privilege and fate
To fall enamoured of the one Muse
Who variously haunts this island earth.

She was your mother, Darien,
And presaged by the darling halcyon bird
Would run green-sleeved along her ridges,
Treading the asphodels and heather-tree
With white feet bare. [200]

Another lovely poem about her is 'The Portrait' which contrasts his muse with those women on whom the Goddess has not descended:

She is wild and innocent, pledged to love
Through all disaster; but those other women
Decry her for a witch or common drab
And glare back when she greets them. [201]

The argument, structure, rhythm and beauty can be seen from the first lines and half of each of its four stanzas, which contrast the muse to other women:

She speaks always in her own voice,
Even to strangers; but ...

She can walk invisibly at noon,
Along the high road; but ...

> She is wild and innocent, pledged to love,
> Through all disaster; but
>
> Here is her portrait, glazing sidelong at me,
> The hair in disarray, ...

Such poetry appears simple, almost natural, but its ease results from Graves' mastery of complexity. Besides the three repetitions of 'She' leading to 'Here' at the beginning of each stanza there is a richness of interior rhymes ('strangers, disaster'), assonance and alliteration ('in her', 'invisibly', 'innocence'; 'disaster', 'disarray'; 'Here', 'her', 'hair'), parallelisms, and other musical and structural harmonies. The second half of the second line of each of the first three stanzas is 'but those other women', then the poem concludes by reversing the focus with the muse asking whether the poet is as different from 'those other men' as she is from 'those other women'.

The poetry hardly needed a specific woman as it was driven by legends and associations from the past, details of which Graves ascribed to the muse. A short poem 'To a Poet in Trouble', which concludes *Poems and Satires 1951*, speaks of a 'Cold Wife and angry mistress' combining with debts to kill him, but it does not matter as the cruel 'Goddess' repays him: 'Your poems now ring true.'[202] He was right: his best poems were usually written at the start of an affair or as an expression of the conflict between being aware that the woman had left him and his need to believe in her love. As a poet now dedicated to the White Goddess what else could he write about except love and its pains? Although limited, and his poetry is limited, his theme was set in a world of magic, legend, literary allusion and myth, and counterpointed with irony, sarcasm and rivals. It resulted in the best body of love poetry of the century, indeed the only interesting love poetry for several centuries without the cynicism of, say, W H Auden's famous 'Lay your sleeping head, my love', in which unfaithfulness and dishonesty are thought basic to being human.

Graves not only needed a muse to whom he could address his poetry, he needed a rival, and Merwin, who was married, became the other man. Merwin's enjoyment of flirting with Judith led to his dismissal and replacement by Martin Seymour-Smith, a admiring young poet and editor. Graves would later claim that Merwin assaulted Judith, the kind of claim he would make about other perceived rivals.

From now on his relationship to his muses followed the structure outlined in *The White Goddess*, including the woman's involvement with a unworthy rival, except that Judith, unlike his later muses, was unwilling to play her role for long. At first she did what Graves thought a muse did. She returned to her lover in Paris, became interested in another man, returned to Deià and lived in Canelluñ, left again for Paris, joined Beryl and Graves in London, moved back to Majorca, this time to Soller where her mother was living, and became engaged. Graves, hearing of her return, took a taxi to Soller, found the young couple in a cinema and started shouting that the man had no right to Judith. The Spanish police, trusting Graves, put the man in jail over night, shortly after which Judith and her fiancé returned to Paris and eventually married.

His unwillingness to accept Judith's leaving him was in his eyes evidence that as a true poet he must try to retain his muse; he kept writing her letters to entice her into doing artwork for a book and inviting her to Canelluñ. Every ruse was used; she was accused of insulting the friendship of himself and Beryl, of not keeping to business agreements, told that her drawings for the book could only be done in Graves' presence, told she had moral obligations. Even after Judith's mother asked him to stop, Beryl was sent to Soller, in the hope that she could entice the now-married Judith to visit him.[203]

This was similar to Graves being sent to bring back Geoffrey Phibbs for Laura. She had always been able to get what she wanted and Graves increasingly was imitating Laura in his treatment of others while creating a Laura-substitute muse. This also was an extension of his behaviour with Peter Johnstone in his idealizing, self-deceiving willingness to be hurt by, and refusal to accept the truth about, the object of his desire. Even bursting into the cinema to declare Judith's fiancé unworthy and having him arrested by the police is analogous to his having forced a Charterhouse teacher into confessing that he had kissed the young man and making him resign. If Graves needed to believe something he was seldom disturbed by reality.

It was by now typical of Graves that everyone, including his wife, was supposed to find ideal qualities in his young muse, even intercede on his behalf, but Beryl, either from prudence, decreasing sexual interest, or remembering his obsessive behaviour with Laura, went along with his wishes and tried to cultivate the young women as friends. She outlasted them.

Graves' new obsession with young women was shaped by the need for some incarnation of the mythology he had created and was certainly driven by his need for poetic inspiration, including the need for conflict as the basis of his writing. The power felt in *Poems and Satires 1951* and *Poems 1953* is fuelled by anger, contempt, and frustration along with love. Besides poems addressed to and about his love there are those, such as the 'The Blue-Fly', which insult, satirize, or attempt to humiliate the other man:

> Five Summer days, five summer nights
> The ignorant, loutish, giddy blue-fly
> Hung without motion on the cling peach
> ...
> Bald head, stage-fairy wings, blear eyes,
> A caved-in chest, hairy black mandibles,
>   Long spindly thighs.[204]

It is the nature of the Muse to be unfaithful and be attracted to disreputable men; there is no clear boundary in the tone of such poems between satire and obsession, between amusement and love. There is a humorous tolerance, an expectation, of being betrayed that is part of the pleasure. 'The Cat-Goddesses' give themselves

> To tatter-eared and slinking alley-toms

No less below the common run of cats
Then they above it; which they do for spite,
To provoke jealousy[205]

'Beauty in Trouble', from *Collected Poems 1955*, offers a
formula which his muses will follow. While applicable to
Judith it became even more true of Robert's relationship to his
second and third muses, Margot and Cindy. The basic story
assumes that women need a 'good angel' as a protector while
loving a 'fiend who beats, betrays, and sponges on her'.

Beauty in trouble flees to the good angel
    On whom she can rely
To pay her cab-fare, run a steaming bath,
    Poultice her bruised eye;[206]

After the good angel pays off her debts and makes her life
comfortable, she becomes bored and returns to 'the fiend'. The
good angel must accept that his only reward will be a sense of
virtue.

Although this is a more amusing poem than 'The Blue-Fly',
Graves, in claiming that 'Beauty' really belongs to 'the evil
angel', is once more implying that women are attracted towards
men who treat them badly. Graves was prone to such women
and saw himself as the good rather than evil angel even when
trying to tempt a woman to leave the man with whom she was
living. For all his pretence at being the protective good angel,
Graves could just as easily be regarded as a seducer obsessed

with possession of the women he wanted. He would try to keep them with money, houses and contact with celebrities, as well as promising that his poetry would make them famous. While Graves' behaviour can be explained in terms of the mythology he created as a foundation for his poetry there was also the lust felt by someone aware he was aging. Most of the poems of this period refer directly to his personal life and each year the number of poems concerned with muses will increase until they dominate his later selected and collected poems. Besides the four generally-recognized muses there were many others who were inspected as possible candidates, such as the attractive Canadian poet Jay Macpherson who was invited to Deià, but turned down an offer to stay on as governess. Although Graves was often generous with young poets she felt he had little time for his children, a view confirmed by his son William's autobiography *Wild Olives: Life in Majorca with Robert Graves*.[207]

Education

Deià still remained a rural village without much contact with the modern world. It was what Graves needed for his work, especially as he often made trips abroad, but the children's education in Deià was a problem. Lucia and Juan were going to the local convent school (girls and boys in separate rooms) and William was being tutored; then in late September 1951 Graves obtained two flats in Palma. He, Beryl and the children had the larger lower flat; Martin Seymour-Smith and his companion Janet de Glanville were installed in the smaller upper one which was used for tutoring William and had a workroom for Graves. For six years Palma would be their home although they returned to Deià on weekends and holidays. Tomás was born in the upstairs Palma flat which had been vacated by Seymour-Smith and Janet. Karl remained in Deià; work to be typed was sent to him on the bus.[208]

Only a school run by French nuns in Palma was willing to take the unbaptized Lucia. Although an improvement over schooling in Deià, it adhered rigidly to the nationalist Catholic view of the world. The students were taught that the expulsion of the Moors and Jews by Ferdinand and Isabella was the model Spain must follow, the Spanish Empire was great, Spanish was superior to other languages – especially English and French – and the Jews could not be trusted and they murdered Christian children. The nuns claimed that the most important quality of a woman was her decency by which they meant that there were no rumours about her sexual life. They also taught that women should be obedient to husbands, that sex was only for procreation, and that most women were frigid. Lessons were dictated to students who had to copy them down and were expected to accept such opinions as unalterable truths.

Lucia and some other girls also went to a classical ballet school three nights a week, which provided relief from the nuns, and offered in their teacher Olga an example of a foreign woman on her own doing something undomestic and earning a living. Lucia admired her and brought her on visits to Deià. Olga, who had enjoyed life during the German occupation of

Latvia, fled the Russians and found herself unable to work in England but welcomed in Spain, would eventually marry an American and move to Ohio.

The Dominican nuns kept warning Lucia that as she had not been christened she risked going to hell when she died. At best God might take pity and leave her in Limbo. There was constant pressure to become a Roman Catholic and eventually a priest asked her to convert without informing her parents. Lucia told her father who said she should wait a year until she was fourteen and then decide. A year later, in 1957, he sent her and Juan to École International in Geneva where instead of Jesus and Franco the young worshipped Elvis Presley, and where she felt a displaced person, an English-speaker whose worst subject was English, with memories of Majorca as home.[209]

During the next few years the education of his two older children by Beryl would become less of a problem. Lucia spent a year in Madrid then in 1961 she would go St Anne's College, Oxford, to study Modern Languages. She would eventually become a translator and writer. In 1954 William was sent to Oundle school; in 1958 he began studying Geology at London University. After graduation he worked in Texas and the Sahara with oil companies, then returned to Deià, married, and for a time managed pension C'an Quet.

Graves now gave up the bottom apartment in Palma, but kept the smaller one for visits, and during the summer of 1957 returned to Deià. Several poems around this time are about the problems of fidelity. 'Woman and Tree' argues that to always love one woman or always sit below the same tree is 'imbecility' and claims the rights of a poet to be a Don Juan, but ends

> To change and chance he took a vow,
>   As he thought fitting. None the less,
> What of a phoenix on the bough,
>   Or a sole woman's fatefulness?[210]

'Call It a Good Marriage' suggests that the sexual aspect of his marriage was no longer satisfying and he would soon look for further muses:

> They acted circumspectly
> And faced the world with pride;
> Thus the hazards of their love-bed
> Were none of our damned business
> Till as jurymen we sat upon
> Two deaths by suicide[211]

He feared growing old and began to suspect he might have prostate cancer. 'The Face in the Mirror' tells of a battered, aging man poised, watching himself, ready to shave, but its real theme is

> He still stands ready, with a boy's presumption,
> To court the queen in her high silk pavilion.[212]

Fame

While Graves was preoccupied by his love life and its relationship to his poetry, he was also becoming a famous writer. There were several collections of writings and new essays, *The Common Asphodel: Collected Essays on Poetry 1922–1949* (1949) and *Occupation Writer* (1950). He was highly productive, publishing more than a book a year, and he was being discovered by a post-war generation of younger writers who rejected modernism, by those attracted towards the wildness and romanticism of *The White Goddess*, by his provocative and outrageous theories, and by Americans who found him good value as a lecturer. He was a much better poet than in the past and even some of his earlier false starts, such as time wasted writing a script for Alexander Korda's 1936 failed film of the Claudius novels starring Charles Laughton, became legendary and was the subject of a BBC television documentary, *The Epic That Never Was* (1965).

Unfortunately a new plan by Vincent Korda, the brother of Alexander, to film the novels involved him once more with the charming Will Price who in 1952, after having proposed Graves write a film script, came to Majorca with his female companion and, heavy drinkers both, ran up hotel and dentist bills of over £500 which Graves had to honour although he was never paid for his work on the script. Price, now supposedly reformed, concocted an impressive scheme which would include himself as producer, Alec Guinness as Claudius, Anna Magnani as Messalina, Ava Gardner as Calpurnia, and Graves himself as Tiberius. The film rights belonged to the estate of

Alexander Korda which Price claimed he could negotiate for, but nothing came of the scheme.[213]

Other visitors to Deià during the summers of 1955 and 1956 included Catherine Nicholson, now Catherine Dalton, the mother of five children and the wife of the Chief Engineer of the Australian Atomic Energy Commission. After her husband's death in 1961 she would play a dramatic role in Graves' later years as she believed her husband's death was somehow inspired by the CIA and other intelligence agencies, a view Graves took seriously.

In England there was a new generation of poets, called The Movement, who championed a British tradition of short, accessible, well-crafted poems in contrast to the internationalism of Eliot and Pound. They claimed Graves' verse as a model of English poetry, although his romanticism and strange mythology were alien to their cool, commonsense pragmatism. Kingsley Amis in 1954 wrote to tell him that he and his friends regarded Graves as the best living English poet.[214]

His Clark Lectures at Trinity College, Cambridge (1954–5) were well attended, drawing poets, critics and scholars from around England, including Sassoon with whom he at last made up. Graves was becoming famous and the lectures would make him more so. He criticized Milton, Dryden and Pope, the canon of great poets who were studied when he was at university. His lecture, 'These Be Your Gods, O Israel!', was a scandal as he attacked Eliot, Auden, Pound and other major 20th-century poets and claimed that their careers proved that they were not real poets as they had not devoted their lives and thoughts to the Muse. While still concerned with the complexities of poetic language and the role of the unconsciousness and psychological conflicts in creation, he now claimed that the value of poetry was in relation to the poet's devotion to the goddess-muse. The foundation for literary judgment should be biography and theme, rather than the formalism common at the time. Although amused by the outrage he caused, he resented that for decades he was regarded by academic opinion as a practitioner of minor, old-fashioned love poetry. He praised minor poets who were his friends, like Siegfried Sassoon and Laura Riding, or poets who had a strong streak of romanticism, like e e cummings, or respected older poetic conventions, like Robert Frost. Despite his rambunctiousness and malice, such poets as Eliot and Auden continued to support him. The lectures were published as *The Crowning Privilege* (1955) along with various essays; the volume was republished by Penguin.

There were awards and invitations to read poetry from many countries. He turned down an offer to be made a Commander of the Order of the British Empire (CBE) in 1957 in the list the Prime Minister, Sir Harold Macmillan, was sending to the Queen. He accepted to give a reading in Israel in 1959 and met Ben Gurion.

Starting in 1957, when he was asked to give three lectures by Mount Holyoke College in Massachusetts, Graves began regularly going on lecture and poetry-reading tours of the United States; these included bookshop appearances, television shows, meeting editors, discussions with publishers and seeing old friends. His American reputation and his finances were suddenly much improved. There were commissions from *The New Yorker*, *Atlantic Monthly* and other prestigious and well-paying magazines. Publishers wanted him and there were different American and British editions of his writings. The miscellaneous prose pieces collected in *Steps* (1958) were mostly first published in well paying American magazines. Some also appear in *5 Pens in Hand* (1958) along with pieces he wrote for British publications. Graves included recent poems in these miscellanies.

The two miscellanies overlap and display the many forms in which Graves wrote. *Steps* consists of short stories, talks, essays, poems, and such 'Studies in History' as 'The Fifth Column at Troy' and 'What Food the Centaurs Ate'. The former argues that the Greeks really conquered Troy because of matriarchal women from Locri, the answer to the latter is hallucinatory mushrooms.[215] The two 'Studies' also appeared in *Five Pens* as 'Historical Anomalies' along with 'The Whitaker Negroes' which would be published elsewhere as a short story. Graves' distinctions between categories and fact and fiction are at times illusory.

He had become a charming writer and lecturer who seemed to inhabit a strange island where customs had not changed for centuries and even the poorest peasant was noble, yet he would without hesitation write of obscure historical texts and mention famous people whom he knew. He apparently had lived fully yet alluded to a code of civilized values which he seemed to hold while mocking bourgeois social, sexual and financial conventions. Graves had become a charming, amusing, eccentric, talented, learned aristocrat as likely to show his familiarity with the latest drug jargon as to claim a direct lineage between the women of some Sicilian village and the pre-patriarchal society that he claimed dominated Europe many thousands of years ago.[216]

Often the crowds were so large that either people had to be turned away or further events scheduled. He defended his views of the White Goddess by saying that even if he were not correct in his claims of a original matriarchy it would not matter as his concern was with poetry and many poets had a similar view of inspiration. Why, he asked, were his claims less legitimate than those of Christians, Jews and other religions. Why is it more foolish to claim a poem is inspired by the White Goddess than to claim that the Hebrew prophets were inspired by God? How can one prove God is a fact?

In a lecture at the New York Young Men's Hebrew Association (YMHA), on 4 February 1957, he claimed that he had not invented a mythology but was tracing its history. 'It is enough for me to quote the myths and give them historical sense: tracing a certain ancient faith through its vicissitudes – from when it was paramount, to when it was driven underground ... In scientific terms, no god at all can be proved to exist, but only beliefs in gods, and the effects of such beliefs on worshippers.' He said that 'A simple loving declaration: "There is none greater in the universe than the Triple-Goddess!" has been made by every Muse-poet in the English language (and by countless others, down the centuries, in various European, African and Asian idioms); though the Goddess is sometimes, of course, given such cautiously abstract titles as "Nature", "Truth", "Beauty", or "Poetry". Myself I think it most unlikely that this grotesque habit will end for a few centuries yet.'[217]

It is difficult to disprove such vague, inclusive claims, but they show his awareness that in recent centuries there has not been a body of devotional and amatory verse about women, and that the energies of romantic poets were directed towards the aesthetic or the sublime in the natural world. Audiences lapped up his romanticism and rebelliousness. He discovered that Americans were generous for tax purposes, his expenses were slight, and he earned more than he expected. A friend might need to accompany him to make certain that his socks matched and that he remembered to have the necessary vaccinations but his eccentricity added to his charm and reputation.

They Hanged My Saintly Billy (1957), his last major novel, is based on the trial of a notorious mid-19th century forger, robber, womanizer and surgeon who Graves thought was not guilty of the murder for which he was hanged. As with most of his fiction it is based on fact, told through many shifts in focus, feels as if it were taking place in the present and is lively reading.

He had also become famous as a translator. Penguin asked him to translate *Transformations of Lucius: Otherwise Known as the Golden Ass* (1950), a work which interested him as myth. Although he disliked the personality and style of Lucan, Graves' translation of his *Pharsalia* (1956) is enjoyable; the Roman's sardonic mock praise matched another side of

Graves' personality, the satirist who was also present inside the romantic poet. *The Anger of Achilles* (1959), his translation of Homer's *The Iliad*, would be given the Italia award. He revised *Good-bye to All That* (1957), improving the style and changing some opinions in keeping with what had happened in recent decades. The revised edition was particularly unflattering to Laura, who now appears as a spider trapping followers to her Covenant.

The decade he and Laura spent in Deià had become a legend. His long withdrawal from the literary world meant that when he appeared again he seemed fresh, new, and indeed many of his best poems were written after 1940. While academics only began to take an interest in him after the dominance of Modernism was fading and they needed new topics of research, it is unlikely that the earlier writing in itself would have stood up to continued analysis as did his White Goddess-influenced poetry. While there was excellent earlier work in both prose and verse, Graves had only become a great writer and major literary figure from the 1940s onward. The many translations, republications of his prose works, controversies, and revising of earlier writings meant that he was now continually part of the literary scene.

He was often brought into contact with the film world and movie stars visited him and became part of his ever increasing network of celebrity acquaintances. Ava Gardner's 1956 visit to Deià included the movie star asking him how to read poetry and his giving her an autographed copy of his earlier Judith poem 'The Portrait'. During the mid-1950s Ingrid Bergman and Roberto Rossellini toyed with making a film of his novel *Homer's Daughter*, but as usual no film was made.[218]

There seemed to be no end of failed attempts to strike it rich by writing for the stage or screen. In 1959 Richard Cohen, an American producer, thought up a Broadway musical about Solomon and Sheba and asked Graves to write the script. Tyrone Guthrie agreed to direct the musical and there was talk of the singer Lena Horne as Sheba, but when she rejected Graves' lyrics the project collapsed. Graves now had a script on his hands and tried to get others interested, including Jerome Robbins and Benjamin Britten, but this was another dead end.[219] Graves did better selling manuscripts; at the end of 1959 the University of Buffalo in New York bought drafts of poems and other materials to go with its Laura Riding collection. He turned down an honorary doctorate from Buffalo but accepted the Gold Medal of the Poetry Society of America. He travelled to New York in January with his daughter Jenny who had proved a favourite of the children by Nancy. She had changed from the hopeless actress and tone-deaf singer of the 1940s to a good journalist, married twice, and was often Robert's eyes, ears and intermediary with the film world. She would die of a brain haemorrhage early in 1964.[220]

There were continuing problems such as naïvety in the company of convivial rogues and con men, but his main problems would be his health and his muses. In his mid-sixties Graves began to have prostate trouble which led to three operations. He was a heavy smoker, a heavy drinker, required large amounts of anaesthetic, and his blood would not clot due to

a form of haemophilia; during the 1959–60 prostate operations he received more than three times the amount of his
own blood which resulted in several small strokes that affected
his brain and caused changes in his personality. Furthermore,
fear of impotence would haunt him in his quest for love and
youth.[221]

9

Three More Muses and Fame

1960–85

Fleeing an unhappy marriage in New York, Margot Callas, a Canadian dancer, worked during the summer of 1959 at C'an Quet, the pension with a beautiful terrace just outside Deià. She wintered in Ibiza and returned to Deià after being asked by Mati Klarwein (1932–2002) – an Israeli painter who was part of the Deià and Ibiza scene – to participate in an 8mm film. After she met Graves that June he decided to appear in the film as a man whom Margot tempts.[222]

Margot would leave and return to Deià many times but she had become Robert's second muse and the subject, in *More Poems 1961*, of the White Goddess poem 'Lyceia':

All the wolves of the forest
Howl for Lyceia
Crowding together
In a close circle,
Tongues a-loll.

As can be seen by such harmonies as the O, L, C sounds and the complex patterns of rhyme – 'howl', 'Ly', 'crowd', 'close', 'loll' – Graves had become a master of sound, but domesticity was boring him and he needed a challenge to keep on edge. He needed discontent and swings of emotion as well as a new woman to desire:

'They learn only envy',
Lyceia answers,
'Envy and hope,
Hope and chagrin.
Would you howl too
In that wolfish circle?'
She laughs as she speaks. [223]

The poem which follows in the volume, 'Symptoms of Love', also written about Margot, describes love as a 'migraine' which blurs vision, blots 'reason', and causes jealousy, but concludes

Take courage, lover!
Could you endure such grief

At any hand but hers?[224]

There was always the need to emphasize the unlikeliness of the woman choosing him and his privileged position when it happens. Many of the poems of the Margot period, such as 'The Visitation', make deft analogies between desire for a woman and poetic inspiration. A further complexity in such a slight lyric is whether the woman (or poem) is really there or merely imagined?

Drowsing in my chair of disbelief
I watch the door as it slowly opens
A trick of the night wind?

Your slender body seems a shaft of moonlight[225]

The poet asks why he has been so lucky to be her choice. Margot was soon involved with Graves' many projects ranging from an annual play performed by friends in Deià to plans to make a film based on *The White Goddess*. Beryl knew it was fruitless to complain; assuming Margot would eventually leave she gave him permission to pursue his new love. At first the relationship was limited to Graves adoring Margot, being in her company, and writing poems about her. 'The Starred Coverlet' praises lovers who have learned 'To lie apart, yet sleep and dream together.'[226] Soon Robert wanted more and, as can be seen in 'Patience' and 'The Falcon Woman', this created problems:

Must it be my task
To assume the mask
Of not desiring what I may not ask?[227]

'Turn of the Moon' and 'The Death-Grapple' imply the relationship became more intimate.

Graves paid for Margot to go to New York to discuss *The White Goddess* film and to seek a divorce. James Reeves' questioning whether Robert was being foolish about Margot resulted in a poem 'Troughs of Sea' beginning "'Do you delude yourself?'" [228] Graves' relationship with Margot was profitable in more than one sense. A sequence of twenty-one love poems earned £250 from the Fifth Guinness Poetry Award for the best poems published in England between July 1960 and June 1961. Included in *More Poems 1961* they would be highly praised by reviewers.[229]

It was three months before she contacted him, and then in a letter co-written with others. By now the choreographer Jerome Robbins was interested in making a film of *The White Goddess* and found Margot suitable. She, however, returned to Europe in the company of Alastair Reid (b 1926), a writer closer to her own age, and the film project fizzled out while the usual scenario would be replayed of the rival man, jealousy and a fickle muse.

As Laura had, as Beryl had with Graves when she was married to Hodge, so his muses had affairs with other men. This was a convention in the Petrachan sonnet sequences of the past where there is always another man who is a rival. Margot understood that Graves was obsessed with her, would not give up his pursuit regardless of her behaviour, and that he would be willing to meet her financial demands. He needed to be humiliated by a heartless, unfaithful muse as a source of his writing; he was using her while she used him.

She returned to Deià, then went to France with Reid. Now everyone had to think Reid a devil. Many excellent *New Poems 1962* resulted including 'Beware, Madam!':

> Beware, madam, of the witty devil,
> The arch intriguer who walks disguised
> In a poet's cloak, his gay tongue oozing evil.[230]

Alastair wrote to say that he loved Margot, and Margot wrote that they were going to Barcelona and Tangier.

Graves had been recommended by the outgoing Professor of Poetry at Oxford, W H Auden, to be Professor for 1961–5. He agreed to stand, was elected, and given rooms at his old college, St John's. Unlike the American tours this lost rather than earned money as he had to pay his travelling expenses from Majorca. As it was necessary to have an MA for the position he was awarded the degree. In his lecture in December, 'The Personal Muse', Graves told his audience that poets might be mistaken in their choice of muse. 'In Her Praise' contrasts the immortal muse with mortal women.

> This they know well: the Goddess yet abides.
> Though each new lovely woman whom she rides,
> ...

Woman is mortal woman. She abides.[231]

He would continue writing to and about Margot who during February 1962 was living in London with Alastair but would not reply.

After not hearing from her for six months Graves threatened to remove his magical protection. To encourage her to return he bought a house, Son Coll, as a present. She now replied she would come to Deià in September and claimed to have finished with Alastair. Beryl, knowing of Margot's plans and trying to avoid being in the way, left for England where Graves was giving further lectures at Oxford and where Lucia began studying at St Anne's College in October 1962. William had found a good job with an oil company.[232] Soon Margot joined Graves, Beryl and Tomás in London.

When Graves returned to Deià Margot flew to Vancouver to see her parents and then to New York supposedly to study photography, after which she was expected in Deià to accompany Robert on a lecture tour of the USA. Graves had been giving her money for the past thirty months and she now needed a 'loan' of £370, which he could not afford and asked from Beryl. In January 1963, Margot again made various requests that cost money, such as paying the rent for her Barcelona apartment, and left for the USA without any forwarding address. In February Graves wrote 'A Last Poem' complaining 'O, when can I give over?' in which he wishes to hear the woman telling him he is her lover. Many poems in *Man Does, Woman Is* (1964) regard inconsistent behaviour as natural to the muse. 'She is No Liar' concludes 'Such things no longer are; this is today'. Instead of coming to Deià Margot flew to London and then back to New York; she cabled asking for more money and Graves offered $500. Her financial dependency made him happy and he wrote 'The Three-Faced', a poem claiming that while the world sees her as inscrutable and self-involved the woman 'has a face of love'.[233]

Graves next saw her in New York where in May 1963 she told him of her friendship with Mike Nichols, the actor, comedian and playwright, whom he soon met and learned that Margot and Nichols were living together. After insulting Nichols, Graves decided that the devotee of a muse had to accept whatever she did.

Back in Deià Graves continued to write long letters to Margot making excuses for her behaviour, but Beryl was fed up with his giving away money, which may have made him think that he needed a muse more likely to bring calm into his life. Others being considered for musehood included Cindy Lee who, ironically, would be the most wild and tempestuous of them. Graves went through months of writing more letters and imagining Margot's return before learning that she had married Nichols. Margot, visiting Palma, asked a friend to think of some compromise between her husband's wish that she return the house Graves had given her and her wish to keep it.[234] Although she was soon replaced by Cindy Lee, Margot kept turning up in Deià, first as an expectant mother, then, 15 months after her marriage, divorced and with a child; but Graves had new muses to pursue.

Mushrooms and Sufiism

Deià was discovered by the Beats and American ex-GIs studying in Europe during the 1950s and in the 1960s was, along with Ibiza, one of the drug capitals of the world (it later became a rock star capital and now a place for celebrities). Graves was influenced by the Sixties in many ways, ranging from his experiments with hallucinogens and a drug-taking muse, to those in his circle who encouraged his ideas about shamans and his disastrous involvement with Idries Shah and Sufiism.

Gordon Wasson, a Wall Street banker, had written to ask Graves about the poisoning of Claudius by mushrooms. Wasson and his wife Valentina were amateur but serious researchers into the history of mushrooms, especially in Russia, and they shared with Graves speculation that ancient cults used hallucinogenic mushrooms as part of their ceremonies. A correspondence developed which would influence the speculation in 'What Food the Centaurs Ate' that hallucinogenic mushrooms were used by ancient Greek cults and were the legendary ambrosia of the gods.[235] After the Wassons returned from Mexico with information, mushrooms and recordings to prove that such mushroom cults were still active, it was inevitable that on a lecture tour in the USA Graves should seek illumination of more than one kind from the Wassons. A small group, including the choreographer Jerome Robbins and Jenny Nicholson, went on an overnight magic mushroom trip on 31 January 1960, while Gordon Wasson played tapes of chanting he brought back from Mexico. For Graves the hallucinations were impressive and he would say that such mushrooms should in future be used at special ritual occasions such as marriage. A second trip several months later using synthetic psilocybin was disappointing and made Beryl ill.[236]

Graves was ambivalent about drugs; he looked down on the drug scene among the foreigners in Deià, but many of his circle of friends were part of that scene and how could he really praise the ancient orgiastic and ritual use of hallucinogens while being snobbish about the now popular use of pot and LSD during a decade when he was trying to keep up with the young and their fashions.

The 'Foreword' to the revised 1960 edition of *The Greek Myths* begins with Graves changing his mind since the 1958 edition; he no longer believed that the many orgies mentioned by the Greeks were solely wine- or ale-induced. 'Centaurs (horse-totem tribesmen), and their Maenad womenfolk, used these brews to wash down mouthfuls of a far stronger drug: namely a raw mushroom, *amanita muscaria*, which induces hallucinations, senseless rioting, prophetic insight, erotic energy, and remarkable muscular strength.'[237] Graves argues that magic mushrooms were the ambrosia mentioned in legends, given to kings, awarded to winners of Olympic contests and which Gordon Wasson rediscovered were used in cult rituals in present-day Mexico. The third edition of *The White Goddess* (1961) removed many earlier references to the occult, while including allusions to drugs, especially magic mushrooms. This edition, the first paperback edition, was popular among the young and brought many to Deià.[238]

Sufiism was another fad of the new decade and during

January 1961 Graves met Idries Shah, who claimed to be an expert on drugs and magic, claimed to be of direct lineage from Muhammad, claimed to know Sufi secrets, and claimed to have access to the original 12th-century manuscript of *The Rubáiyyát of Omar Khayyám*. Graves wrote a 'Foreword' to Idries' *The Sufis* (1964). Idries offered him a transcription of the supposed original *Rubáiyyát* which he said was a Sufi work in the possession of his family. Graves made a poetic version, although he had no knowledge of the original, its language, its history, and its author. He did not even know that the *Rubáiyyát* is not a long poem but consists of unlinked short lyrics which Victorian translators had tried to unify with an implied story. After his version of *The Rubáiyyát of Omar Khayyám* (1967) was savagely reviewed, Graves foolishly continued to defend Idries, even after learning that the transcription was based on a Victorian translation. While it is possible to regard such misplaced loyalty as a result of ageing and the effects of his operations, Graves long had a history, as shown by his accepting Laura Riding as a prophet, of unquestioned faith in those who were tricking and using him. He also had a history of vigorously arguing in favour of his assertions. He suspected that he had been tricked although he never admitted he was wrong. It was under the influence of Idries' Sufiism that he wrote *Mammon and the Black Goddess* (1965), claiming that after unquestioningly accepting the trials sent by the White Goddess, a poet enters the higher service of the Black Goddess.

Man of letters

Now in international demand for poetry readings and lectures, Graves continued his annual lecture and poetry-reading tours to the USA including a 1961 lecture to the American Academy and Institute on his interpretation of the Arabic word 'baraka' (blessing or spiritual wisdom), which he picked up from the Shahs and which in his view became the essential element of poetry. He went to Greece to participate in a television programme on Greek myths. His 1962 Oxford lectures concerned technique and vulgarity (the term Laura and Stein used for what they disliked). Five lectures were published as *Oxford Addresses on Poetry* (1962). The 1963 lectures concerned the Black Goddess. Perhaps the bravest lecture was in 1963 at Massachusetts Institute of Technology where he defended the idea of poetic trances, of poetic thought and the irrational, and asked that the audience accept his views as true in their own way as any other beliefs. He was selective about his honours, refusing being made Companion of Literature by the Royal Society of Literature (1962). His later Oxford lectures can be found in *Poetic Craft and Principle* (1967).

Publication of translations and retelling of mythology continued with, for Penguin, *The Hebrew Myths* (1964) co-authored by Raphael Patai. This used similar methods to those in *The Greek Myths*. Although Graves distinguished Hebrew myths from Greek, with the former serving nationalist and monotheistic purposes, he still saw earlier pre-biblical traces of matriarchy and goddess worship. As he became a popular name among the literate he published several illustrated books for children. These included *The Penny Fiddle: Poems for Children* (Cassell 1960), *The Siege and Fall of Troy* (1962), *The Big Green Book* (1962) which was illustrated by Maurice Sendak, and *Ann at Highwood Hall* (1964).

While he often seemed resentful and dismissive of the famous modernist poets, he was generous to those less well known, especially from the former colonies. When Jonathan Cape mailed an early copy of Derek Walcott's first book of poems, *In a Green Night* (1962), Graves replied 'Derek Walcott handles English with a closer understanding of its inner magic than most (if not any) of his English-born contemporaries', a quotation still found on book jackets of Walcott's poems.[239] Walcott (b 1930), from St Lucia, became one of the world's best poets and was awarded the Nobel Prize for Literature in 1992.

Keki N Daruwalla was stunned to receive praise from Graves, who enjoyed a poem in *POET*, an Indian literary journal founded in Madras edited by Krishna Srinivas. Graves wrote admiringly of the poem's wild energy and said that the Indian goddess Kali had inspired Daruwalla, who would also discover the Black Goddess (1 May 1965). Graves wrote again from Canelluñ in December claiming that every true poet knows when he has written a true poem and does not need editorial comment. He criticized Tagore and surprisingly revealed knowledge of Indian poetry in translation. He also wrote that he once knew the 'President' of India who still remembers him. Other letters followed (April 1966, 15 July 1967 and 24 July 1970), usually commenting on some poem of Daruwalla's or expressing views about marriage being a patriarchal institution or the sources of legends. The final letter, after being sent Daruwalla's first book *Under Orion* (1970), was eventually used as a blurb for Daruwalla's fourth volume of poetry *Winter Poems* (1980).[240] Keki N Daruwalla (b 1937) became one of the better Indian poets writing in English; his *Collected Poems 1970–2005* was published by Penguin in 2006.

Cindy

His third muse was Cindy Lee, a wild drug-user who bled Graves financially while dividing her affections among other men. While hoping that Cindy would be his Black Goddess of contentment, his poems of this period are sometimes bitter about love and even sex; he continued to be driven by unsatisfied emotions.

They first met in New York where Cindy was among the circle of Americans who summered in Deià. He was moaning about Margot but Cindy had her eye on him and when she first came to Deià in 1963, Graves paid her expenses. She was in her mid-30s, bright, hated to make plans, enjoyed sex, knew how to use her attractiveness, was worldly-wise and soon was having an affair both with Graves and with John de St Jorre, who had resigned from the Foreign Office to become a writer, each of whom was delighted by her inventiveness in bed. During October she followed Graves to England where, meeting Idries Shah, she claimed that her mother was Mexican and her real name was Emil Laraçuen.[241] With a few other twists her name became Amelia Maria-Theresa Laraçuen which to my ears combines echoes of Amaliae (Amy) von Ranke Graves, Robert's mother, and Laura. Her unpredictability delighted Graves, who decided that as Emil she was the peaceful Black Goddess he deserved after the pains of devotion to the White Goddess. He obviously enjoyed people who invented their past and themselves.

Increasingly Graves seemed to live in a fantasized world of charms, magic, omens and, after Cindy returned to New York, supposed telepathy. She travelled to Arizona and then Mexico where she claimed to have cousins and became Aemile, then came back to New York supposedly to pursue a career as a painter.

Such comings and goings were common to many of Graves' new friends, the international drug-taking bohemia of the 1960s who, along with the ex-GI painters, now dominated Deià social life, especially during the summer. Graves sought renewal in this culture. During February 1964 he stayed in New York in Greenwich Village with the musician John Benson Brooks, a friend he shared with Cindy/Aemile. The couple met jazz musicians, went to a jam session, and Graves introduced Cindy to Alec Guinness. 'The Green Castle' with its 'seventh heaven, trance of love', and Adam rediscovering Eve, reveals his elated feelings at the time.[242] On their way back to Deià they stayed with Ava Gardner in Madrid where they had four nights of partying. The famous actress impressed Cindy, who would write to her complaining of Deià although admiring Graves' ability to bring excitement into her life.

Feeling renewed, Graves thought he had found his Black Goddess with whom he would forever be happy and began contemplating leaving Beryl and the children, and following Cindy wherever she wanted to go. Even Cindy had more sense and knew that he was too old and unwilling to age gracefully. He needed Beryl to take care of him. Cindy in Deià was bored, often tripping on LSD, would welcome Robert's attention, then mock him to friends. The world of famous people and strange ideas he represented attracted her enough to play with thoughts of marrying him, but this was mostly talk although he took it seriously. She is the 'Firm-lipped, high-bosomed, slender Queen of Beanstalk Land' in 'Batxóca':

> By what outrageous freak of dissimilarity
> Were you forced, noble Batxóca, to fall so deep in love
> With me as to demand marriage[243]

His feelings for Cindy dominate *Love Respelt* (1965), a slim volume of limited circulation that she illustrated, published for his 70th birthday.

This was the peak of their relationship; from now on it would be downhill and Cindy would change from the Black Goddess to yet another of Robert's fleeing, deceiving muses, one with a need and appetite for the money he could provide. After she returned to New York she stopped writing to him. By July he learned that she was living with and planning to marry a former lover, Howard Hart. This began a pattern in which Cindy would promise to return to Deià and, on Graves' money, travel with Hart. She wrote in September 1964 saying she would return and instead flew to an alpine village in France with her lover. Graves kept fruitlessly writing and sending her telegrams. After he sent more money she met him and Beryl for a few days in Paris mid-October, then he took Cindy to London where she would stay at the house of an airline hostess who had lived in Deià. Graves rejoined Beryl in Oxford for his first lecture of the term.

Cindy enjoyed being with him in London but soon went, on his money again, to live with Hart in Paris. By December she and Hart had quarrelled and she was back in London. Graves was pleased. Once more he deceived himself into thinking Cindy wanted him permanently rather than as a source of funds and a refuge between adventures. He told friends that he was going to leave Beryl and follow Cindy to Mexico or wherever she wanted. He even told Beryl. Although he had bought Cindy a ticket to New York where he planned to meet her, she again disappeared until January 1965 when he learned she had been living in London with Hart. Graves kept making excuses for her, telling people that her behaviour could be explained by feelings of guilt. Cindy left London for Paris and then New York with Graves following, having told Beryl they were finished; deciding he would write no more books, Robert fired his long-time secretary Karl. He and Cindy went to Puerto Vallarta in Mexico where she had numerous affairs and Graves, leaving her with a lot of money among her pot-smoking friends, returned to Deià alone, but carrying marijuana. Beryl greeted him without comment and soon he was thinking that once her Mexican adventure had finished he would team up with Cindy again.[244]

She turned up in New York in June 1965 after having been jailed in Mexico on drugs charges; she also wrote to Graves telling him he should leave Deià. He asked her to come to Deià for his 70th birthday in July; being once more short of money she agreed. She was there in August when Lucia married her jazz drummer boyfriend Ramon Farran. Beryl refused to be friendly with Cindy and would stay in bed whenever she was in the house. William and his wife disliked her, and soon Cindy was high on drugs, wild at parties, and returned to London. Graves was his usual self, telling people that he and Cindy were an eternal couple.[245]

In his first two Oxford lectures of 1965 he discussed what made a good muse and these were often Cindy's characteristics, such as a lack of ethical values and an unwillingness to be possessed by a husband. The poet risks everything in his pride of celebrating the muse. Graves denied that this was masochism or stupidity.

Interest in Graves extended to his past and the failed filming of the Claudius novels, the subject of *The Epic That Never Was*, a BBC TV documentary broadcast during June in which Graves himself appeared and which included all the surviving footage from 1937.

The musician John Benson Brooks wrote in May that Cindy arrived a day late for a luncheon engagement, was tripping on LSD and happy with Hart. She continued to write to Graves who, feeling that she needed further encouragement, gave her copyright to his letters. Using the $37,000 from sales to the University of Southern Illinois of some of his letters and drafts of poems, he bought a house, C'an Susanna, which later became Torre Susanna, for Cindy on the foolish assumption that once she had a house she would settle in Deià. When she did not come it was nicknamed Withering Heights. After putting some money aside to pay Karl, he sent most of the remaining money, over $20,000, for her to buy a house in Puerto Vallarta where he continued to assume they would live together. Hearing she was hospitalized in New York he sent more money; the cause was an overdose of sleeping pills.[246]

Graves' behaviour was even more foolish than it appears as during this period he was without money from royalties. He and other well-known English writers had a scheme, created by Graham Greene, to avoid British taxes by selling their copyrights to a Swiss firm which would then pass royalties to them. This worked from 1962 until 1965 when the middleman was caught distributing forged money and all his assets were frozen. Antonia Dalton, Graves' granddaughter, told me at the time that he had lost all his money. That was an exaggeration but between needing to hire a lawyer and other expenses he lost money before he could see his royalties again.

He kept saying that his marriage with Beryl was over, although Cindy was once more living with Hart. She wrote him (27 September 1966), that he was too old for her. A second letter from Puerto Vallarta told him that she was living with Hart in the house Graves had bought. A third letter in which she praised Hart led to him replying that their relationship was at an end, although if she were in trouble he would help. It was, of course, not the end, and she continued writing and asked for $500 for an emergency, which he sent. Many of her letters still spoke of love, but some mentioned Hart, and Graves sent her presents.

Graves had a major series of operations; the first in 1959–60 required three operations for prostate cancer, the second series of three during 1971 and 1972 was on his nose for leaking sinuses. There was also an operation to remove his gall bladder in 1966. It was during the prostate cancer operations that he gained his fourth and least harmful muse. While fruitlessly hoping to regain Cindy he began courting Juli Simon, a dancer and daughter of his English friends George and Simona Simon. Although she was the most innocent and least experienced of his muses, even Juli would find herself pushed by him into temptation and betrayal.

Cindy and Juli

Juli(a) had been raised in a family who had a high opinion of Graves, had stood with him during some of the crises in his life, who had a room specially prepared and waiting for him when he visited London, and who often went to Majorca. Graves was the godfather of her older sister, who first attracted Graves; Helena admired him but had no amatory interest, but while he was nearly dead in hospital Julia, then 17, declared her love, a declaration that she asked him to keep from her parents. She soon became his 'Juli', although in poems addressed to her she remained Julia. She first came to Deià the summer of 1966 and soon Graves was writing poetry about her.

Although claiming to be painfully devoted to his muses, he was not above courting more than one at a time. He would mention Juli in letters to Cindy in the hope of regaining her. While it is unlikely that anything he wrote would have influenced Cindy, the boast that Juli was still a virgin allowed the more experienced muse to argue that Juli was not really in love with him. She stung him by claiming he never really loved her and the poems he wrote about her were false.[247] As Graves was unwilling to give up his hopes for Cindy while Juli admired him, he went through elaborate contortions of persuasion and devotion, some of which appear more like farce than sources of romantic poetry.

For a time Cindy seemed content as Graves helped with the sale of over 400 letters he had written to her since 1960.[248] He insisted that her letters to him be added as he wanted the future to know the full story and he absurdly hoped that Cindy would purchase an annuity and pursue her talents as an artist rather than smuggle drugs across the border. Then in June 1968 Cindy returned to Deià; after Graves housed her in a cottage he owned, she began drinking heavily and spreading rumours about Juli. Catherine Dalton, his daughter by Nancy, became fed up with Cindy, was stunned to learn that she had almost destroyed his marriage to Beryl, and threatened to kill her if she did not leave Deià.

Cindy did but as usual chaos followed. There was a cable saying she was returning, then a letter informing Graves that she had another lover in New York, Peter Weismiller. When she came to Deià with him they were put up at the same cottage which Catherine (who had since left) had forced her to leave. Peter then left for India, she moved to Paris, and there was a problem resulting from the $12,000 which she received from the sale of the letters to the University of Victoria. She had been paid in advance but had not signed over copyright to the university. She was now going to India where she planned to buy semi-precious stones to sell in Europe. In June 1969 there was continued anxiety about her whereabouts and the assigning of the copyright for the letters. Graves kept saying it would all work out, but he had lost contact with her once more, although he thought she had returned to Paris. After much trouble, in August she was found and the copyright assigned, which was followed by accusatory letters from Cindy asking Graves for more money. Cindy and Weismiller went to California where he had a mental collapse, thought he was Jesus, and received electric-shock treatment. Graves would occasionally hear from or of her in such places as Puerto Vallarta and Nepal, until 1972 when he refused to send her money in Turkey.[249] With Graves no longer willing to be a cash cow that was the end of his third muse and, belatedly, his main share of the 1960s.

Juli

Juli was far less of a problem although, being young and discovering life, even she would at times shake the illusions which Graves constructed about his muses and, increasingly, the world. His mind was going, although at this point it was difficult to know what was age and what his usual eccentricity. Juli was a good muse for someone in his state, undemanding and sentimental. She was a ballet dancer and Graves would travel to her performances.

Perhaps because he saw her as young and innocent the poems, such as 'Virgin Mirror' addressed to her in *Poems 1968–70* feel more like exercises than really charged with feeling:

> Souls in virginity joined together
>   rest unassailable:
> Ours is no undulant fierce rutting fever [250]

This is an attempt at the tight-knit logic of early 17th-century poetry, a model also followed in such vocabulary as the contrast between the unusual 'undulant' and the striking 'rutting fever' of which his poetry of this period could use a bit more. 'How It Started' tells of a teenage dance in Deià. Asked by her to join them:

> In the circumstances I stayed away
> Until you fetched me out on the tiled floor
> Where, acting as an honorary teen-ager,
> I kicked off both my shoes. [251]

Earlier, in 1968 on the 50th anniversary of his first marriage

Graves had written to Nancy Nicholson to make peace, which lasted until her death in 1977. Perhaps he was through with the excesses of the past and really did want a Black Goddess for a peaceful old age. He had been affected by his operations and in a pre-Viagra era he was probably past it. The poems could use more conflict and emotion. 'Brief Reunion' celebrates having 'inbred faculties far wiser/ than any carnal sense' while recalling the 'carnal pains' that had seized him and Juli,

> Three summers past in a burst of moonlight,
> Making us more possessive of each other
> That either dared concede?[252]

The next poem in the sequence, 'The Judges' tells of him and 'Julia' innocently arguing over shells at the beach. 'Love and Night' and 'Child with Veteran' claim that the contrast in their ages may shock others but not them. They kiss and write letters to each other.

Juli, however, was a normal young woman who in her twenties acted like most women of her age during the 1960s and 1970s, and there were at least two occasions when she and Graves temporarily clashed over her love-life. One was in late 1969, the morning that he came knocking on our door looking for Juli while knowing she was probably sleeping with Robert Page. As Juli's experimentation was known among Graves' friends it seems likely that Page was set up as a needed rival. Juli was living in Torre Susannah across from us and Graves suggested that she put up Page and Sonja Guy, whom he was to marry. Page and Sonja had been quarrelling so it was not surprising that he and Juli had a fling and even thought of going away together. 'Purification' tells the tale with the woman confessing:

"He numbed my heart, he stole away my truth,
He laid hands on my body.
Never had I known ecstasy like that:
I could have flown with him to the world's end
And thought of you no more."[253]

The poem concludes with the woman purifying herself by bathing, but it seems an odd topic for a poem, and it was not the last occasion when Graves felt he had a rival.

Although Graves went through his routine of claiming that his muse's unfaithfulness was the worst shock of his life, he no longer kept up his frenzied sufferings and was soon back to writing calm, inoffensive poetry. Graves was now in decline and his time of greatness over. Another incident occurred during 1972. He would soon become too senile for Juli to pretend to be his muse. This created difficulties; when she returned to her house in Deià, he would insist on seeing and badgering her.

Influence and aging

Honours came his way. Deià officially made him an adopted son. He was invited to the Olympic Games in Mexico City and given a Gold Medal for a poem in Spanish. On his return he was awarded the Queen's Medal for Poetry in England and also invited by PEN Hungary in 1968 to visit Budapest (which in 1969 instituted a Robert Graves Prize), followed by a trip to Russia, which Beryl enjoyed and would revisit but he found dull. He would revisit Hungary in May 1970 with Catherine for a poetry congress. The Mermaid Theatre in London held 'Poetry: an Evening with Robert Graves' on 6 September. Later, in October, he and Beryl would go to Belgrade, invited for a International Writers Conference. He was back in Budapest, invited by PEN, in May 1971. The many trips by Graves and Beryl, and sometimes by Beryl alone, to Eastern Europe were a way to spend royalties earned from translations of his books. Although he continued to write poetry, the prose finished with some collected miscellanies, interviews, and other bits and pieces in *The Crane Bag* (1969), *On Poetry: Collected Talks and Essays* (1969) and *Difficult Questions, Easy Answers* (1972).

His influence and contacts during the last decades of his life can be seen in his role in the repeal of a new British law making it an offence to have offered for rent a house in which drugs were used. Stephanie Sweet, a former student of Spanish at Oxford who was working at the Ashmolean, had during a holiday sublet to other students an Oxfordshire farmhouse sublet to her by a farmer who had leased it from Oxford(!). The police thought one student was a drug dealer, and charged Sweet with 'managing premises where drugs have been used'. Lucia Graves knew Stephanie at Oxford and brought the case to the attention of her father; Stephanie then moved to Majorca where she supported herself by teaching English. Graves wrote an influential article for the *Times* in 1968 and the case took on national importance; the Law Lords ruled against the new law and its new category of absolute offences. The case was soon discussed in legal textbooks. Sweet moved on to North Africa where, after beginning as a language teacher, she worked her way up to become British Consul in Tangier, and was awarded an MBE.

Graves was less successful in defending his translation of the *Rubáiyyát* and whenever he asked the Shah brothers about the manuscript they had excuses for not producing the manuscript or evidence that the original they had used for their crib existed. A scholar who found the head of the Shah family in Afghanistan was told that no such Jan Fishan Khan manuscript existed and indeed the man had never heard of Omar Khayyám. By this time Graves did not have the intellectual energy to reply to his critics. Mental deterioration was taking its toll. The foolishness concerning his *Rubáiyyát* translation would cause many to feel that his seemingly brilliant insights elsewhere were not to be trusted.

The operations during 1971–2 directly contributed to the mental confusion and senility that became obvious as he aged, although he remained physically impressive for a few years, still scaling the cliff from his house to the small rocky beach in Deià. The two operations on his nose during which he was heavily anaesthetized affected his memory and beginning in 1972 he found concentration increasingly difficult and slow. His behaviour became irrational. Made an Honorary Fellow of St John's in 1973 he complained about an American book dealer never having paid him for the manuscripts he sent to Buffalo. He was wrong and had to apologize.

In 1972 *I, Claudius* and *Claudius the God* were adapted for the stage by John Mortimer for a short run in London with David Warner as Claudius; discussion of a television adaptation of the novels soon followed, which led to a highly successful 13-episode series in 1976 which brought Graves' name to the general public and contributed further to his new fame. The BBC was said to have spent £800,000 on the series. The royalties were useful in providing care for him in his old age.

After two decades of working with Schuyler Jackson on her never-finished dictionary intended to teach the world the real significance of words, Laura Riding reappeared. There was a 1962 BBC 'Introduction for a Broadcast', an expanded version which appeared in the American magazine *Chelsea* in 1964. Her major work, 'The Telling', was published in *Chelsea* during 1967 and, expanded, as a book also titled *The Telling* (1972). *Chelsea* devoted issues to her writing in 1976 and in 2001 after her death.

Laura was irked by Graves' success and wanted to claim her role in making him a poet, literary critic, and theorist. In 1970 she initiated a long correspondence with the famous literary critic and poet William Empson; it started by complaining that while he acknowledged a debt to Graves he had ignored her, particularly her role in the 1927 *A Survey of Modernist Poetry*. Her main reappearance in Graves' life was a long article she published in the Winter 1974 *Denver Quarterly* rejecting unflattering remarks in the revised *Good-bye to All That*, telling her side of her life with Graves, and claiming for herself much that he had written then including the ideas that went into *The White Goddess*. She was always good at publicity, and a Riding revival was in progress with scholars choosing sides. A period of reconciliation began. In his Oxford lectures Graves admitted that Laura was more influential on his work than implied by the revised *Good-bye to All That*.

In 1974 the Royal Welch Fusiliers made him guest of honour at a dinner in London. While he was delighted by the invitation his conversation lacked direction and he wandered into a stranger's car expecting to be taken home.[254] His last public readings began in September 1974 in Warsaw where he was invited by the Polish Writers Union. On arrival he began talking about a German sign he had read during the First World War, replied to an interviewer's question about Greek myths by talking about LSD and mushrooms, and at a book signing kept asking where he was. He and Beryl went on to Budapest where Graves claimed to have been in Rome during the Second World War. He read without trouble in Krakow but became lost during a visit to the market. This was his last poetry-reading tour.[255]

By 1975 Graves was senile, often lost, and likely to cause incidents. John Montague arranged for him, with Beryl, to visit Cork and Dublin, in May 1975, but Graves would forget what he read and read a poem twice. His creative and public lives were over. As his 80th birthday approached there were various celebrations including a one-day show at the Royal Court in

London. At St John's College in June where a new building was opened with a 'Robert Graves' room to house material about him, he appeared badly dressed but well behaved at a dinner honoring him; however in London at a lunch for the cast of the televised *I, Claudius* he claimed to be 140 years old. When the series was televised he watched it and had no idea of his relationship to it. In July at his 80th birthday party in Deià there was a reading of his poems at which he accused the reader of plagiarism.[256] He did write a poem for Juli, however, his last poem.

He was suffering from Alzheimer's disease. From 1976 he could not be left alone and was sometimes violent. He was incapable of recognizing or remembering much and kept imagining he was back in the Wimbledon of his childhood or in the trenches during the Great War. Each year his condition became worse. He would start talking in German and seemed unable to understand how to climb stairs. During 1978 he began losing physical co-ordination and fell.

Beryl had been the foundation of the marriage, keeping it going long after others would have given up. By conventional standards Graves was an impossible husband, but she was loyal and his writing and contacts provided a remarkably interesting life. She seemed bewildered by his behaviour now and often saved the day by treating his incomprehension and senility as amusing eccentricities. She never really accepted that he would not return to better mental health and until his death she kept Canelluñ open to their friends. Juli, who now had a daughter and a house in Deià, would sit by him and he somehow knew she was there.

He died on 7 December 1985. By this time the strange Englishman who had come to Deià in 1929 was internationally famous and the village considered him an honoured son. The strongest young men in the village carried his coffin and he was buried in the Deià churchyard on a hill above the village.

Graves was a remarkable person who lived at times an unbelievable life. He had two wives, each of whom had four children, and a brilliant if deranged poet mistress who dominated and humiliated him for over a decade. Although he was long disgusted by sexual desire, he bedded many women. He worked on his writing every day and by the time of his death had written, edited or co-authored over 140 books including such classics as *Good-bye to All That* and the two Claudius novels. He was a brilliant, imaginative, eccentric and pig-headed scholar. His wild *The White Goddess* may be often wrong but is an accurate metaphor for a process of inspiration that good poets know. It is a work of genius but I would not build anything on its foundations. His life was dedicated to being a poet: even his love of and humiliation by women was part of a scenario he needed to write emotionally charged poetry. While his monument is his poetry, many authors would feel complete to have written his novels and other prose works, and to have known and been known by so many famous contemporaries.

10

Afterlife, Afterthoughts

S oon after Graves was buried in the local Deià churchyard, a memorial service was held in London. While he
had never been someone like T S Eliot, W H Auden or
Allen Ginsberg who seemed to epitomize a literary and cultural
movement, his novels sold well, poets praised his work, and
during the final decades of his life he received the recognition
that goes with becoming part of the literary canon. He became
representative of other literary and cultural movements that
had been neglected, such as the First World War poets, the
non-political writers of the 1930s, the forerunners of recent
feminist thought, and those writers who had created their own
mythologies.

Besides the quality of his writing there were cultural
reasons for this increased stature. Modernism and its great
writers, such as Eliot, Lawrence and Auden, were increasingly
being attacked or ignored by later generations, while Graves
was now thought neglected and his short poems were seen as
among the best of the century. The interpretive tools he had

provided, such as *The White Goddess* and his Trinity College and Oxford lectures, taught how to appreciate his work.

His romanticism and interdisciplinary way of thinking were now fashionable. *The White Goddess* became a foundational text for 'Neo-Pagans' and 'Wiccans' as well as part of the history of the first wave of feminist research. Its virtuoso scholarship and insight turned pre-history into history for feminists and those seeking a goddess-centered spirituality. The idea that the White Goddess is the actual muse of poetry influenced Ted Hughes' *Shakespeare and the Goddess of Complete Being* (1992) and the studies in mythology offered by Joseph Campbell who, in *The Power of Myth* (1988), still carried on the speculative cultural anthropology that influenced Harrison and Graves.

After half a century when the impersonality of great art had been an aesthetic credo, Graves inspired those who saw art as personal – about the artist's life and beliefs rather than the condition of society and culture – yet within a tradition of muse-given poetry. The transformation of Graves' Goddess from prehistoric deity to poetic muse influenced Derek Walcott's drama *Dream on Monkey Mountain* (1970), where the White Goddess is not only the muse of poetry, but specifically of the white European poetic tradition that Walcott hoped to conquer. She is the unattainable whiteness that drives the central character into temporary madness, an image of black racial rage at being excluded. Influenced by Graves, Walcott extended the figure of the white moon, a romantic symbol for poetic inspiration, to a literary and cultural tradition to which he, a black man, initially felt an outsider and had to accommodate.[257]

Many of Graves' views were current when he was young and remain present in the intellectual world, although they are minority opinions. It is still common to regard Greek theatre and even Shakespeare's plays in terms of myth, ritual or their psychological counterparts. *Hamlet* seems based on rituals of the sacrificial king and the Oedipus complex.

His exegesis of the Bible for occulted historical narratives was a continuation of an older school of biblical studies, a formerly influential movement which argued that the original Jewish Christians saw Jesus as human, a leader of the Jews with claims to the Jewish throne. The Pauline church transformed Jesus into a Greek sacrificial god whose reality was mystical rather than political. This contributed to the expansion of Christianity beyond the Jews.

Because of Graves' close attention to details of poetry and especially its many possible resonances he is also regarded, along with Laura Riding, as one of the founders of the New Criticism and Practical Criticism, two important schools of literary analysis during the second third of the last century.

Centenary, war poets, 1960s

Interest in Graves was strong in 1995, the centenary of his birth, which coincided with the first decade since his death. Arcane published *Robert Graves: The Centenary Selected Poems*, edited by Patrick Quinn. Carcanet also inaugurated its massive Robert

Graves project, which includes over 20 volumes of his works. That year also saw a new enlarged version of Martin Seymour-Smith's biography, the concluding volumes of Richard Perceval Graves' three-volume life, his important edition of the 1929 *Good-bye to All That*, and Miranda Seymour's biography. There were major international conferences on Graves studies held in Palma and at St John's College Oxford. An association of Graves scholars was formed with annual conferences and the journal *Gravesiana*.

Another stimulus was the renewal of interest in the First World War and its writers, especially Sassoon. In the TV documentary *1914–1918* (1996, American title *The Great War and the Shaping of the 20th Century*) Michael York performed the role of Robert Graves. Graves' writings are mentioned in such TV documentaries as *Drug Taking and the Arts* (1994) which look at the 1960s.

Biographies

Although Graves claimed that his life could be found in his poetry, little was known of his life beyond the early years covered in his autobiographical, at times misleading, *Good-bye to All That* until the publication of Martin Seymour-Smith's *Robert Graves: His Life and Work* (1982). It was only after the monumental three-volume biography by Graves' nephew was published that it became possible to see the life in detail. It might seem that not much was left to discover but Miranda Seymour's *Robert Graves: Life on the Edge* (1995) came up with valuable information not found in his nephew's three volumes as well as offering a more critical perspective than Graves' other biographers.

The three biographies were written by those outside the university world. Graves was a major literary figure who did not easily fit into the schema taught by universities of Georgians or War Poets followed by Modernists, followed by Left writers of the 1930s, followed by a Modernist-influenced 1940/50s' traditionalism, the Beats, postcolonialism and so on. Although he was well represented in most anthologies of poetry the academy came to him late. He remains an outsider although it should have been possible to see his work through such perspectives as modernism, psychology, mythology, feminism and postcolonialism.

Homosexuality

Parts of Graves' life were unknown, could not be written about, or were not understood, until the people involved died. That his affectionate interest in other men continued after he left Charterhouse and into his first marriage was not well known or documented until Siegfried Sassoon's diaries and Graves' letters of that period were published. With recent research into gay history, more is known about such friends as Robbie Ross, Sassoon and Marsh and their role in the cultural and political life of England. Graves tried to dismiss this part of his past as it troubled him but it influenced his relationship with women and his mythology of the female deity. Was the early homosexuality, the wish to be dominated by women, and the mythology, brought about by his relationship to his mother?

Interpretation and evaluation

The monumental autobiographical and interpretative edifice Graves spent most of his life erecting stands in the way of other perspectives. Critical studies of Graves' writing are all influenced (as I have been) by *Good-bye to All That*, *The White Goddess*, *The Greek Myths* and similar works which provide handy keys to unlock the significance of the poems and prose. In building upon its predecessors, each book of literary criticism continues the process. Miranda Seymour's *Life on the Edge* hints at other directions that might be taken when she claims that Laura Riding had a history of hysteria and when she suggests that Graves had already invented the psychodrama he wanted to perform with women and that Laura became his victim, taken to Majorca from which she wanted to escape. She understood what Graves wanted and why; each of the muses was given her lines by Graves. There are other aspects of this story that need thinking about, such as the hedonism and aggressive public unconventionality that begins in Graves' life once Laura becomes part of it. There were already signs of it after the failure of *Country Sentiment* and of the shop at Boars Hill; by 1926 Graves appears to have withdrawn from and quarrelled with everyone.

Then there is the question of what is Graves' best poetry and why. Robert Richman's review article, 'The Poetry of

Robert Graves', in *The New Criterion*, argues that rather than the myth of the White Goddess being the source of Graves' best poetry it limited his range and the resonances of his later verse.[258] If there is only one story worth telling it soon results in repeatedly thin versions without metaphoric timbre. Richman claims that the later poetry is literal, lacks symbols; the muse is addressed directly rather than evoked. Richman prefers such earlier poetry as 'Like Snow', 'The Pier Glass', 'The Cool Web', 'The Terraced Valley', 'Love in Barrenness'. He says that early in life Graves had a 'terror of reality' instilled by his parents and he used Riding and the mythology of the White Goddess to protect himself from the nastiness of the world. In such poems as 'Through Nightmare', 'On Portents' and 'The Cool Web' Graves examined his fears of the modern world. Richman offers an alternative approach to his life and work that needs considering.

There are still other ways of looking at Graves beyond his love life, fears, invention of a mythology, and biography. He had a sense of humour, was often amusing, and could be a good social satirist as in 'Sirocco at Deyá' in which the hot summer wind blowing through the village provides a natural setting for the deadly gossip within such an enclosed community:

> While slanderous tongues in the small cafés
> And in the tightly-shuttered limestone houses
> Clack defamation, incite and invite
> Knives to consummate their near-murders ...[259]

Graves dismissed his non-goddess poetry but many of his better poems are amusing and satirical, even comic.

Periods

The trouble with limiting Graves to the poet of the White Goddess is that his life and writing were varied. I have tried to show that there were such distinct periods as the somewhat socially maladjusted youth who had strong religious and patriotic beliefs that conflicted with his homoerotic feelings at least into his early twenties; then there was the physically and mentally wounded ex-soldier who rejected the Victorian values of his past without replacing them by any authority and whose life was influenced by studying psychology and cultural anthropology, by marrying inappropriately, by believing in matriarchy and socialism, who was influenced by Mallick's relativism, and who foolishly hoped to support himself and his family through writing best-selling volumes of poetry. Such confusion ended when he met Laura who broke down his sexual inhibitions and allowed him to believe that she was perfect. She disciplined him into a major writer while allowing him to perform the masochistic subservience that he needed. Then there is the time with Beryl of the writing of *The White Goddess* and the goddess poems which are an ultimate mythology, a stage beyond and a replacement for Laura's now-lost infallibility. And then there is the period of the first three muses in which the White Goddess mythology was used to justify claims that the women who attracted Graves were her temporary incarnations. Increasingly they became the foolishness of a famous but ageing man. And that was followed by the Black Goddess, his last muse, and senility.

There is no reason why any period of his life necessarily led to what happened next. Suppose Sassoon had agreed to go to Egypt with Robert and Nancy before Laura Riding was invited? It is unlikely that Sassoon would have become his idolized muse living with him in Majorca. Indeed if Laura had not jumped from that window it is unlikely that she and Robert would have ever needed refuge in Deià. Other lives for Robert Graves were possible which would have resulted in a different body of poetry.

Deià

Contemporary Deià consists of about 750 people many of whom are foreigners in residence or foreigners who live there part of the year. It is twice the size of the isolated rural village which greeted Graves with indifference, although it continues to see him as a source of money. His Deià home, Canelluñ, is now correctly called Ca n'Alluny and is a national monument open to tourists. There is a Robert Graves school in Deià. He has become part of international culture brought to the attention of the same tourists who visit Valdemossa to see where George Sand and Chopin spent a winter. Deià is now famous and has often been described in newspaper and magazine articles as the most beautiful place in the world; it has an annual chamber music festival and is the home of world-famous celebrities, internationally-advertised boutique hotels, and restaurants listed in the Michelin food guide. There is a Deià walking tour which also attracts those interested in keeping fit during their holidays. Tourists to Deià can visit the Seizin Press, which has been resurrected as a publishing house by Tomás Graves.

Some of the tourists, however, may be less interested in Graves' life and work than in the hotel suite where Princess Diana stayed (it has a private swimming pool), the many rock stars such as Robert Wyatt and Kevin Ayers who lived in Deià, or the bar where Mick Jagger jammed. Celebrities with Deià homes include Michael Douglas and Richard Branson; movies continue to be filmed there.

The immediate post-war invasion by GIs, tourists and hippies has itself become a legendary period which scholars try in vain to keep distinct from Graves. Robert's nephew and biographer R P Graves, when writing of the late 1960s in Deià says, as others have of that period, that if you were not there you can not believe what it was like.

Archaeological museum

There was more to Graves' Deià in the 1960s than wild muses, such progressive rock groups as The Soft Machine and Gong, Daevid Allen and David Solomon's *The Marijuana Papers* (he also edited *Drugs and Sexuality* and *The Coca Leaf and Cocaine*) and an American college's year abroad programme that had to be closed after a visiting dean found the students and faculty all stoned. Graves was interested in and helped support the Deià Archeological Museum founded in 1962 by Bill Waldren (1924–2003), an attractive reconversion of an ancient mill, which contained the finds from the many digs by Waldren and friends. The museum is one of the attractions of Deià for tourists. As Graves had his own mythology about the pre-history of the Mediterranean, research into the possible astronomical and ritual significance of objects from the Bell Beaker Culture, besides their major archeological significance, could support his own theories.

Waldren, one of the American post-war GIs who found their way to Paris and then Deià, was for a time an Action Painter, but his discovery of caves containing a previously unknown ancient culture in Majorca led to his becoming an archaeologist. Although he left high school before graduation to become a professional ice skater he was later granted a B Litt by Oxford University which allowed him to write a doctoral dissertation on his discoveries and he was soon associated with the Pitt Rivers Museum and teaching Mediterranean pre-history at Oxford part of the year. So while Graves invented Deià's prehistory he also helped towards recovering the island's actual archaeological past.

Afterthoughts

Like many who rebelled against social convention and Victorian values after the First World War, Graves claimed to be living by a new honesty in keeping with what he felt rather than ideas. But more than honesty, he wanted a leader to replace the values he had given up. He left Nancy for Laura because Laura was assured and demanding whereas Nancy lacked direction. It is unfortunate that his need for authority after a period of relativism parallels political developments in Europe between the wars. While he hated Fascism and Communism his writings show a similar concern with heroes and heroism and a distrust of liberal democracy. *Good-bye to All That* and his novels are about heroism.

Graves wanted a leader while wanting to lead. You needed to belong to his party. Each woman he chose was a test for his friends who were required to agree to his evaluation of the woman or lose his friendship. And the test became increasingly more difficult – Nancy, Laura, Cindy.

His early life displays many signs of a homosexual dominated by an imposing mother, but his father was no bully, was not violent, and indeed Robert resented him for his willingness to help him, a willingness which the then-unsuccessful son regarded as an attempt at domination through kindness. Although *Good-bye to All That* suggests that Graves hated his father ever since he was sent to Charterhouse, there is little evidence of such a dislike before the Islip period when the failure of the shop created large debts that Robert and Nancy could not pay. Until then most of Robert's references to his father are affectionately dismissive of him as old-fashioned. It was the mess he was making of his life at the time (and his father's comparative success) and his subsequent liaison with Laura that drove son and father apart.

Graves the house-husband might be explained by his theories of matriarchy, but his willingness to be humiliated by Laura and his muses derived from deeper impulses than ideas about women during ancient times. His early homosexual leanings were never fully resolved and accepted; he increasingly pretended that they never occurred. How else can one explain him saying during the 1950s to an American artist in Deià, 'You and I, Jimmy, as ex-boxers and front line soldiers could never be suspected of homosexuality.'[260] In the 'Foreword' to *The White Goddess* there is a strange remark when Graves claims that Platonic homosexuality is worse than sodomy because it is an 'intellectual' attempt to reject the requirement that man give homage to the goddess through women.[261] This is the reverse of his earlier disgust with sex and insistence that homosexuality should be Platonic. Graves could not hide his past from himself.

An even more curious version of this argument can be found in the notes about Ganymede in *The Greek Myths* which claim that originally male sodomy was a form of goddess worship in which men emasculated themselves and dressed like women. Sodomitic priests were an institution in the temples of the Great Goddess, until the Greeks turned philosophy into an intellectual game that did not require a ritual goddess. 'With the spread of Platonic philosophy the hitherto intellectually dominant Greek woman degenerated into an unpaid worker and breeder of children wherever Zeus and Apollo were the ruling gods.'[262]

In his relationships with women, what begins as lust and

love turns into a desire to be dominated and self-destructive behaviour. Being humiliated was what Graves expected from his pursuit of women, but it seem clear that he manipulated his humiliations and could change his affections from one woman to another when he wished; indeed he could, as with Cindy and Juli, have two muses at once. The pattern of mad love followed by masochism, as the woman rejected him for a rival, and his seemingly crazed attempts to be loved again, was a scenario that he created and followed and had women play. It was a version of the mythology he claimed for the White Goddess with her destruction of her lovers.

Such a mythology and his re-enactment of the story enabled him to write poetry, but why did he need this drama, how did it start? His tense relationship with his demanding mother was transformed into a script where love for a domineering woman led to a partial reversal of gender roles, his humiliation, and need to further humiliate himself in trying to regain the woman's love. He claimed that the goddess took her son as a lover, that Zeus was really the child of the goddess and she turned herself into his wife to make him unhappy for his rebellion against her. There is his script.

Looking back over Graves' life and writing what seems his desire to be superior, controlling and distinctive, conflicted with a need to belong, to love, to be controlled. Boxing for a time gave him a way to feel pain and sexual excitement, to win and to bond. He kept trying to form enclosed communities with lovers and friends but they seldom gave satisfaction. His novels, instead of notating society, are stuffed with learning.

There is no intimacy, no sensuality or love. Love is treated in a perfunctory manner, something said to exist but never portrayed or imagined. The prose works are concerned with survival, pain, heroism and winning. The world of Graves' novels is driven by insecurities, resentments and egotism, except for a tiny minority, usually the narrators, who live by notions of honour, patriotism or blind faith. Such values are abstract. Whether at Charterhouse or in the army or in his relationships with men, or marriage with Nancy or his relationship with Laura and his muses, Graves wanted to bond while feeling antagonistic towards others, as he also needed the tension of insecurity and partial rejection.

He imagined a bi-polar world of father/mother, aesthetes/bullies, 'so'/not 'so', soldiers/civilians, old/young, imagination/reason, true poets/Apollonian poets, science/poetry, poetry/hack writing, his circle of friends/others, Freud/Rivers, Majorca/England, Oxford/Cambridge, Royal Welch Fusiliers/other regiments, scholars/himself, matriarchy/patriarchy, and goddess worship/other religions.

Good-bye to All That and *The White Goddess* are like his relationships to Nancy, Laura and his other muses, in allowing him to create worlds in which he was at the centre and the only true believer while others, even his closest friends, fail to accept his word about the truth. Thus he had to invent or cause quarrels with his father, Sassoon, Phibbs and others. It is reductive to look for one cause but the insecurity of his relationship to his mother while being part of a large family is the probable starting place.

If Graves likes to appear the ultimate outsider and loner he was part of his time, indeed one of those who helped define it whether in his complaints against and revelations of homosexuality at public school, his story of the Great War and the disillusionments that followed, or even in his myth-making, a trait he shared with other major modern poets such as Yeats, Stevens and Eliot who felt the need of a spiritual or philosophical system. What is odd is that his mythology offers a form of the Oedipal struggle in which father. and son fight for the mother.

When he was young his mother impressed on him and his sisters the importance of culture and especially of poetry. His mother put together a poetry magazine to which the children contributed. It was perhaps to please his mother that he became a poet. But why claim that his father did not help him and was his rival? One needs to look ahead to *The White Goddess*:

> The Theme, briefly, is the antique story, which falls into thirteen chapters and an epilogue of the birth, life, death and resurrection of the God of the Waxing Year; the central chapters concern the God's losing battle with the God of the Waning Year for the love of the capricious and all-powerful Threefold Goddess, their mother, bride, and layer-out.[263]

In other words the one theme of all the world's mythology and true poetry concerns rivalry for and incest with the mother who is all women. Graves, however, explains this differently as the poet identifies with the God of the Waxing Year and his 'rival is his blood brother, his other self, his weird'. This suggests an incestuous battle, which explains Graves' demonizing his rivals, even his rivalry with his brother Charles. Whether the other man is father, brother, or another poet does not matter, life is competition between the old and the new. Significantly he discovered the White Goddess mythology after losing Nancy and Laura to other men and having won Beryl from Hodge. The White Goddess mythology also gave him a way to transcend his fear of death; as long as he chased, praised and possessed women he shared in an eternal timeless process.

Modernism evolved out of late Romanticism and shared many of its tastes such as being attracted towards primitive culture and a dislike of 18th-century poetry. Although Graves invented a different kind of Romanticism based on worshipping women rather than nature, he was one of the antimodernist moderns; an artist who continued to create within traditional conventions of his craft, while in outlook and life he was part of a radical revolt against the social, moral and spiritual boundaries in which he was raised and educated. In his writing such features of 20th-century thought as psychoanalysis and cultural anthropology take other, radical directions. Besides being an excellent poet and a major literary figure he deserves his own niche in the history of modern culture.

How good a poet was he? Where does he rank among 20th-century English poets? Eliot, Auden, Yeats, Wallace Stevens and a few others created influential new styles, which Graves never did, and their writings had deeper cultural resonances. Graves was a consciously minor poet, someone who avoided in his verse the major themes and changes in form which characterized the major poets of the past century. The skepticism and disillusionment which might have gone into his verse went into his novels. If I say he was a great minor poet it would be in keeping with his aims as he had no wish to write large-scale poems of major significance and he preferred short personal lyrics.

There is, however, never any agreement on rankings. If I say T S Eliot was a better poet I can hear recent voices arguing that Eliot was not a great poet. If I acknowledge Graves' limitations, too many love poems and many of them sentimental, but claim his best poems had a greater harmony and intensity of language and some were more amusing than, say, those of W H Auden, I know poets whom I respect who claim Auden was the greatest poet of the past century. Let us say Graves was one of the best ten poets writing in English when he was in his stride. You can decide on the other nine.

Notes

Abbreviations

AH   Richard Perceval Graves, *Robert Graves, The Assault Heroic 1895–1925* (Weidenfeld and Nicolson, London: 1988).

BI   *In Broken Images: Selected Correspondence of Robert Graves 1914–1946*, ed Paul O'Prey (1982) (Moyer Bell, Mt Kisco, New York: 1988).

CB   Robert Graves, *Count Belisarius* (1938) (Penguin, Harmondsworth: 1954).

CP   Robert Graves, *The Complete Poems in One Volume*, eds Beryl Graves and Dunstan Ward (Penguin, London: 2003).

DB   Deborah Baker, *In Extremis: The Life of Laura Riding* (Grove Press, NY: 1993).

GB   Robert Graves, *Good-Bye to All That: An Autobiography*. ed with a Biographical Essay and Annotations by Richard Perceval Graves (Berghahn Books, Providence and Oxford: 1995).

GM   Robert Graves, *The Greek Myths*, 2 v (Penguin, London: 1977).

IC   Robert Graves, *I, Claudius* (Penguin, Harmondsworth: 1970).

MS   Miranda Seymour, *Robert Graves: Life on the Edge* (Transworld, London: 1996).

RP   Richard Perceval Graves, *Robert Graves and the White Goddess 1940–1985* (Phoenix, London: 1998).

SS   Martin Seymour-Smith, *Robert Graves: His Life and Works* (Abacus, London: 1983).

WG   Robert Graves, *The White Goddess*, ed Grevel Lindrop (Carcanet, Manchester: 1997).

YL   Richard Perceval Graves, *Robert Graves, The Years with Laura 1926–1940* (Viking, New York: 1990).

Chapter 1

1. SS pp 454–5; MS p 336.

2. GB pp 265–7, 370. The 1957 edition of GB is clearer about the danger.
3. Lucia Graves, *A Woman Unknown* (1999) (Counterpoint, NY: 2001) p 148.

Chapter 2

4. GB 'Introduction' and 'Annotations'.
5. GB pp 10, 11.
6. http://www.gravesfa.org/gen068.htm.
7. AH pp 25, 17.
8. MS pp 13–14.
9. GB pp 12–13, 36.
10. AH pp x–xv depicts family trees of the Graves and Rankes.
11. AH pp 38–9, 47, 49, 51.
12. GB p 11.
13. GB p 18.
14. GB pp 26–7, 36–7.
15. GB p 30.
16. MS pp 307, 11–12; GB p 37.
17. MS p 14.
18. GB pp 53, 43; CB p 9.
19. AH pp 231–2, 280.
20. GB pp 19, 24, 25.
21. GB pp 23–7; AH pp 50–9.
22. GB p 52.
23. GB pp 14, 19; MS p 15; AH p 56.
24. AH pp 106, 104.
25. GB p 51.
26. MS p 35; AH p 77.
27. AH pp 37, 39, 51.
28. BI p 317; AH pp 76–7, 71–2.
29. GB p 57.
30. GB p 58.
31. AH p 88; MS p 27; GB p 58.
32. GB pp 59–60.
33. BI p 90.
34. SS pp 119, 501.

Chapter 3

35. AH p 110.
36. CP p 11.
37. AH pp 118, 119.
38. MS p 41.
39. AH pp 127, 129, 130.
40. CP p 20.
41. CP p 14.
42. CP p 7.
43. SS p 74.
44. BI p 48; MS p 45.
45. BI pp 50–1; AH p 148.
46. BI pp 59–60; AH p 159.
47. Simon Brittan, 'Graves' "Myth of Skelton"', *Gravesiana*, 1.3 (June 1997) pp 251–72.
48. CP p 689.
49. CP p 20.
50. CP p 27.
51. Chris Baldick, *The Modern Movement 1910–1940* (Oxford University Press: 2004) p 336.
52. CP p 26.
53. MS p 65; GB p 25; George Robb, *British Culture and the First World War* (Palgrave, NY: 2002) p 57.
54. AH p 186.
55. CP pp 32–3.
56. CP p 32.
57. CP p 31.
58. CP pp 31, 47; BI pp 82–4 (13 September 1917); MS p 67.
59. BI pp 68 (to Sassoon 21 April 1917), 89 (to Nichols November 1917); AH p 186.
60. AH p 190; BI p 100 (28 July 1918).
61. Jodie Medd, 'The Cult of the Clitoris', *Modernism/Modernity*, 9.1 (January 2002) pp 21–49. For the nurse see GB p 220. GB 1957 edition gives her name as Marjorie.
62. BI p 103.
63. GB p 242.
64. BI p 207; GB p 363.
65. CP p 807; BI p 94.

Chapter 4

66. AH p 219.
67. SS p 87.
68. AH pp 225–6.
69. BI p 150.
70. *Siegfried Sassoon Diaries 1920–1922*, ed Rupert Hart Davis (Faber, London: 1981) pp 74, 91, 150, 162, 288, hereafter *Sassoon Diaries*; BI pp 203, 225–33.
71. GB p 271.
72. SS p 89; AH pp 229, 243.
73. AH p 242.
74. AH pp 243, 246.
75. AH p 243.
76. *Sassoon Diaries*, pp 90, 103.
77. AH p 217.
78. CP p 71.
79. CP pp 78–9.
80. CP p 77.
81. CP p 71.
82. CP pp 101, 103, 104, 108.
83. CP p 129.
84. CP p 122.
85. CP p 124.
86. CP p 126.
87. CP p 142.
88. AH p 53.
89. GB p 281.
90. Madhuri Santanam Sondhi and Mary Walker, 'Basanta Kumar Mallik and Robert Graves: Personal Encounters & Processes in Socio-Cultural Thought', *Gravesiana* 1.2 (December 1996) pp 109–46, esp pp 126–33; and AH pp 276–7.
91. CP pp 252–3.
92. MS p 125; AH p 309.

Chapter 5

93. DB p 28; MS p 132.
94. GB p 294.
95. CP p 283.
96. MS p 142.

97. MS p 156; SS pp 142–3.
98. SS p 143.
99. MS p 147.
100. MS pp 153, 155.
101. SS p 145.
102. MS pp 157–8.
103. CP p 314.
104. MS p 164.
105. MS pp 166–8; DB p 106.
106. DB p 154.
107. DB pp 235–7.
108. DB p 106.
109. MS p 170.
110. MS pp 173–5.
111. BI p 190 (to Marsh 16 June 1929); MS pp 176–7.
112. MS p 178.
113. DB p 155.
114. Baldick, *The Modern Movement 1910–1940*, pp 265, 342.
115. GB p 322.
116. MS p 180.
117. Details in GB; BI p 209 (2 March 1930).
118. GB p 154.
119. GB p 221.
120. Christopher MacLachlan, 'Heroes and Hero-worship in *Goodbye to All That*', *Focus on Robert Graves and His Contemporaries* 1.8 (November 1988) pp 8–12.
121. GB pp 110–11.
122. GB pp 130–1.
123. GB p 174.

Chapter 6

124. Kingsley Amis, 'Graves in Deyá', *Gravesiana* 1.3 (June 1997) p 245.
125. MS p 207.
126. MS p 193.
127. CP p 295.
128. DB p 234.
129. DB p 239.
130. DB p 237; MS pp 200–2.
131. DB p 238.

132. YL p 219; MS p 224.
133. YL p 206; BI pp 224–5.
134. BI pp 220–9.
135. DB p 159; SS p 133.
136. CP p 285.
137. CP p 296.
138. CP p 298.
139. CP p 309.
140. CP p 304.
141. CP p 334.
142. CP p 337.
143. CP p 338.
144. CP p 338.
145. CP p 340.
146. Robert Graves, *Antigua, Penny, Puce* (1936) (Penguin, Harmondsworth: 1984) p 17.
147. Robert Graves 'Legends of the Bible', *Steps* (Cassell, London: 1958) p 206.
148. IC pp 24–5.
149. IC p 196.
150. IC p 144.
151. YL p 218.
152. YL p 212.
153. SS p 242.
154. YL pp 246–7.
155. MS pp 256–7.
156. YL p 248.
157. MS p 260.
158. CB p 147.
159. CB p 421.
160. MS p 259.
161. YL pp 286–7.
162. BI p 273.
163. SS pp 320–1.
164. Laura Riding and Robert Graves, 'From a Private Correspondence on Reality', *Essays from 'Epilogue'*, ed Mark Jacobs (Carcanet, Manchester: 2001) p 164. First published in *Epilogue 3* (1937) pp 107–30.

Chapter 7

165. Robert Graves and Alan Hodge, *The Long Weekend* (Faber, London: 1940; 2nd impression: 1950) pp 200, 201, 437.

166. BI pp 289, 292, 293.
167. Robert Graves, 'Foreward' *Sergeant Lamb of the Ninth* (Methuen, London: 1940; 2nd ed: 1945) p v.
168. Graves, *Sergeant Lamb*, p 38.
169. Graves, *Sergeant Lamb*, pp 38–9.
170. Graves, *Sergeant Lamb*, p 69.
171. MS pp 290–1.
172. CP p 402.
173. RP p 34.
174. RP pp 35, 79–80.
175. Robert Graves, 'The Ghost of Milton', *The Crowning Privilege* (Pelican: 1955) p 342.
176. BI p 320 (4 December 1943).
177. Robert Graves, *Hercules, My Shipmate* (Pyramid, New York: 1966) p 21.
178. Graves, *Hercules, My Shipmate*, p 25.
179. RP pp 87, 101.
180. CP p 398.
181. WG pp 19–20.
182. CP pp 405, 406.
183. CP p 405.
184. WG p 5.
185. RP p 115.
186. BI p 337.
187. RP pp 85, 116–17.
188. RP pp 45, 103–4.

Chapter 8

189. CP p 428.
190. WG p 6 (1997).
191. MS pp 346, 347.
192. GM vol 1 'Introduction' pp 12, 13.
193. GM vol 1, pp 13, 22.
194. GM v 1, pp 36–7.
195. RP pp 141–2, 146–7.
196. RP p 148.
197. CP p 429; RP p 162.
198. RP pp 157, 221.
199. CP p 458.
200. CP p 438; PR pp 175–7.

201. CP p 437.
202. CP p 444.
203. SS pp 336–7.
204. CP pp 454–5.
205. CP p 454.
206. CP p 463.
207. SS pp 337–8; William Graves, *Wild Olives: Life in Majorca with Robert Graves* (Pimlico Press, London: 1995); 2nd ed (Vintage, NY: 2001).
208. RP p 199.
209. Lucia Graves, *A Woman Unknown*, pp 62, 67–8, 108–9.
210. CP p 476.
211. CP p 482.
212. CP p 470.
213. SS pp 452, 484–5.
214. MS p 343.
215. Robert Graves, 'The Fifth Column at Troy' and 'What Food the Centaurs Ate', *Steps* pp 265–74 and 319–43.
216. For example, his review 'Maenads, Junkies and Others', *Steps* pp 189–95; 'The Fifth Column at Troy', *Steps* pp 265–74 and *Five Pens in Hand* pp 289–98.
217. WG 1997 ed Appendix B pp 496, 503.
218. SS pp 464–5; RP pp 246–8.
219. SS pp 486–9.
220. SS p 506; MS p 384.
221. MS pp 381–2.

Chapter 9

222. RP p 311.
223. CP pp 496, 497.
224. CP p 497.
225. CP p 498.
226. CP p 501.
227. CP p 502.
228. CP p 500.
229. Bruce King, *Derek Walcott: A Caribbean Life* (Oxford UP: 2000) pp 177–8.
230. CP p 525.
231. CP p 524.
232. RP pp 346, 352, 354.

233. CP pp 535, 534, 538.
234. RP p 373.
235. Graves, *Steps*, pp 319–43.
236. RP pp 300–2, 306.
237. GM vol 1 'Foreword', p 9.
238. WG ' Introduction', pp xvii-xviii.
239. King, *Derek Walcott: A Caribbean Life*, p 181.
240. Emails from K N Daruwalla to author, 18 January 2007; 26 February 2008. Daruwalla sent me photocopies of five letters; another is mislaid.
241. RP pp 377–8, 381.
242. CP pp 546–7.
243. CP p 563.
244. RP pp 406, 408.
245. RP pp 414–15.
246. RP pp 417, 425, 428; MS pp 432–3.
247. RP p 448.
248. RP p 449.
249. RP pp 457, 461, 475.
250. CP p 639.
251. CP p 640.
252. CP p 641.
253. CP p 645.
254. MS pp 456, 457.
255. RP p 486.
256. RP p 488; MS pp 458, 459.

Chapter 10

257. King, *Derek Walcott: A Caribbean Life*, pp 154, 249–50.
258. Robert Richman, 'The Poetry of Robert Graves', *The New Criterion* 7.2 (October 1988) [www/newcrierion.com/archive/07/oct88/richman.htm]
259. CP p 460.
260. Roy Skodnick, 'James Metcalf Joins the Smoky Smiths: Deya-Paris-Santa Clara del Cobre', *Gravesiana* 1.2 (December 1996) p 195.
261. WG p 7.
262. GM vol 1, p 117.
263. WG p 20.

List of
Robert Graves' Works

As Graves wrote, edited and translated over 140 books – including 55 volumes of poetry and 20 books of fiction – as well as contributing to others, this is a selected bibliography mostly of works mentioned in this biography. They are marked P (poetry), F (fiction), E (essays and literary criticism), M (miscellanies), T (translations), and A (anthologies, works edited, selected works of others). Works co-written or co-edited are marked *. Place of first publication is London unless otherwise noted.

P *Over the Brazier* (Poetry Bookshop: 1916).

P *Goliath and David* (Charles Whittingham: 1917).

P *Fairies and Fusiliers* (William Heinemann: 1917).

P *Treasure Box* (Chiswick Press: 1920) illustrated by Nancy Nicholson.

P *Country Sentiment* (Martin Secker: 1920).

P *The Pier-Glass* (Martin Secker: 1921).

E *On English Poetry: Being An Irregular Approach to the Psychology of This Art* (William Heinemann: 1922).

P *Whipperginny* (William Heinemann: 1923).

P & F *Mock Beggar Hall* (Hogarth Press: 1924).

P *The Marmosite's Miscellany* by 'John Doyle' (Hogarth Press: 1925).

P *John Kemp's Wager: A Ballad Opera* (Basil Blackwell: 1925).

P *Welchman's Hose* (The Fleuron: 1925).

E *Contemporary Techniques of Poetry: A Political Analogy* (Hogarth Press: 1925).

F *My Head! My Head! being the history of Elisha and the Shunamite woman; with the history of Moses as Elisha related it, and her questions put to him* (Martin Secker: 1925).

E *Poetic Unreason and Other Studies* (Cecil Palmer: 1925).

E *Another Future for Poetry* (Hogarth Press: 1926).

E *Impenetrability: or, the proper habit of English* (Hogarth Press: 1926).

P *Poems 1924–26* (William Heinemann: 1927).

A *John Skelton (Laureate)* (Ernest Benn: 1927).

E *Lawrence and the Arabs* (Jonathan Cape, 1927).

E *The English Ballad: A Short Critical Survey* (Ernest Benn: 1927).

E* *A Survey of Modernist Poetry* (William Heinemann: 1927) co-authored by Laura Riding.

E* *A Pamphlet Against Anthologies* (Jonathan Cape: 1928) co-authored by Laura Riding.

P *Poems 1929* (Seizin Press: 1929).

F *The Shout* (Matthews & Marrot: 1929).

P *Ten Poems More* (Hours Press, Paris: 1930).

M *But It Still Goes On: An Accumulation* (Jonathan Cape: 1931).

P *To Whom Else?* (Seizin Press, Deià: 1931).

P *Poems 1926–30* (William Heinemann: 1931).

P *Poems 1930–1933* (Arthur Barker: 1933).

F *The Real David Copperfield* (Arthur Barker: 1933).

F *I, Claudius* (Arthur Barker: 1934).

F *Claudius the God and his Wife Messalina* (Arthur Barker: 1935).

F *Antigua, Penny, Puce* (Seizin Press, Deià, and Constable: 1936).

F *Count Belisarius* (Cassell: 1938).

P *Collected Poems* (Cassell: 1938).

E *T E Lawrence to His Biographer Robert Graves* (Doubleday, NY: 1938).

P *No More Ghosts* (Faber: 1940).

F *Sergeant Lamb of the Ninth* (Methuen: 1940).

F *Proceed, Sergeant Lamb* (Methuen: 1941).

E* *The Long Weekend* (Faber: 1940) with Alan Hodge.

P* *Work in Hand* (Hogarth Press: 1942) with Alan Hodge and Norman Cameron.

E* *The Reader Over Your Shoulder* (Jonathan Cape: 1943) with Alan Hodge.

F *The Story of Mary Powell: Wife to Mr Milton* (Cassell: 1943).

F *The Golden Fleece* (Cassell: 1944) [USA: *Hercules, My Shipmate*].

F *King Jesus* (Cassell: 1946).

P *Collected Poems 1938–45* (Cassell: 1946).

P *Collected Poems 1914–1947* (Cassell: 1948).

E *The White Goddess: a historical grammar of poetic myth* (Faber: 1948).

E *The Common Asphodel: Collected Essays on Poetry 1922–1949* (Hamish Hamilton: 1949).

F *Seven Days in New Crete* (Cassell: 1949) [USA: *Watch the North Wind Rise*].

M *Occupation Writer* (Creative Age Press, New York: 1950).

T *Transformations of Lucius: Otherwise Known as the Golden Ass* (Penguin: 1950).

F *The Isles of Unwisdom* (Cassell: 1950).

P *Poems and Satires 1951* (Cassell: 1951).

P *Poems 1953* (Cassell: 1953).

P *Collected Poems 1955* (Doubleday Doran, New York: 1955).

E* *The Nazarene Gospel Restored* (Cassell: 1953) with Joshua Podro.

T *The Greek Myths* (Penguin: 1955) 2 vols.

F *Homer's Daughter* (Cassell: 1955).

T *Winter in Majorca* (Cassell: 1956).

T *Twelve Caesars* (Penguin: 1956).

T *Pharsalia* (Penguin: 1956).

E* *Jesus in Rome: a historical conjecture* (Cassell: 1957) with Joshua Podro.

E *Goodbye to All That* revised (Cassell: 1957).

F *They Hanged My Saintly Billy* (Cassell: 1957).

M *Steps: stories, talks, essays, poems* (Cassell: 1958).

M *5 Pens in Hand* (Doubleday, Garden City: 1958).

E *The Crowning Privilege: The Clark Lectures 1954–55* (Pelican: 1959).

P *Collected Poems 1959* (Cassell: 1959).

T *The Anger of Achilles: Homer's Iliad* (Doubleday, NY: 1959).

P *The Penny Fiddle: Poems for Children* (Cassell: 1960).

P *More Poems 1961* (Cassell: 1961).

E *The White Goddess* revised (Faber: 1961).

P *New Poems 1962* (Cassell: 1962).

E *Oxford Addresses on Poetry* (Cassell: 1962).

P *The Siege and Fall of Troy* (Cassell: 1962).

P *The Big Green Book* (Cromwell-Collier, NY: 1962) illustrated by Maurice Sendak.

P *Man Does, Woman Is* (Cassell: 1964).

P *Ann at Highwood Hall* (Cassell: 1964).

T* *The Hebrew Myths* (Cassell: 1964) co-authored by Raphael Patai.

F *Collected Short Stories* (Cassell: 1965).

E *Majorca Observed* (Cassell: 1965).

E *Mammon and the Black Goddess* (Cassell: 1965).

P *Love Respelt* (Cassell: 1965).

T* *The Rubáiyyát of Omar Khayyám* (Cassell: 1967) with Omar Ali-Shah.

E *Poetic Craft and Principle* (Cassell: 1967).

M *The Crane Bag* (Cassell: 1969).

E *On Poetry: Collected Talks and Essays* (Doubleday, New York: 1969).

P *Poems 1968–70* (Cassell: 1970).

P *Poems 1970–1972* (Cassell: 1972).

M *Difficult Questions, Easy Answers* (Cassell: 1972).

T *Song of Songs: text and commentary* (Collins: 1973).

P *Collected Poems, 1975* (Cassell: 1975).

Further Reading

Web sites

Many Graves archives are available through http://homes.ukoin.ac.uk/~lispjh/graves/

His diaries 1935–9 and much else can be found on the web site of St John's College Robert Graves Trust. www.robert-graves.org/sjcarc.php

For more information about and photographs of Deià see www.info-mallorca.co.uk/deia/ or www.deia-mallorca.com/uk/index.htm or deià.info/indexen.html

Biographies and autobiography

Martin Seymour-Smith's *Robert Graves: His Life and Work* (Hutchinson: 1983; pb Abacus: 1983), written by a friend of the poet, tends to defend Graves' every action. The second edition (1995), published after Graves' death, is less cautious in discussing Laura Riding and others. Richard Perceval Graves' monumental three-volume biography is of immense value for its detail – *The Assault Heroic 1895–1926* (Weidenfeld & Nicolson: 1986), *The Years with Laura 1926–1940* (Viking: 1990) and *Robert Graves and the White Goddess 1940–1985*

(Weidenfeld and Nicolson: 1995). More analytical is Miranda Seymour's *Robert Graves: Life on the Edge* (Doubleday: 1995; pb Doubleday: 1996). I am especially indebted to R P Graves and Miranda Seymour for many facts and insights.

Richard Perceval Graves' edition of *Good-bye to All That: An Autobiography* (Berghahn Books, Providence & Oxford: 1995) prints the complete 1929 text for the first time, shows where it differs from the 1957 version, and has a valuable biographical essay about the original context. Annotations include those by Sassoon and others.

Conversations with Robert Graves, ed Frank Kersnowski (University Press of Mississippi: 1989) contains interviews and memoirs.

Editions

A uniform edition of Graves' major works is being published by Carcanet Press, Manchester. It includes three volumes of his *Complete Poems* (edited and annotated by Beryl Graves and Dunstan Ward). There is also a one-volume edition (2000). The Penguin Classics *Complete Poems* (2003) consists of the Carcanet volumes without notes.

Carcanet has also published the *Complete Short Stories* (ed Lucia Graves: 1995); *Collected Writings on Poetry* (ed Paul O'Prey: 1995); *The White Goddess* (ed Grevel Lindrop: 1997); *The Sergeant Lamb Novels* (ed Patrick Quinn: 1999); *The Greek Myths* (eds Patrick Quinn and Michel Pharand: 2001); and *The Hebrew Myths* (ed Patrick Quinn: 2005). *Some Speculations on Literature, History and Religion* (ed Patrick Quinn: 2001) ranges from Graves' first to his last published essay.

Many Carcanet volumes republish two or more works together: *Homer's Daughter* and *The Anger of Achilles* (ed Ian Firla: 2001); *Antigua, Penny, Puce* and *They Hanged my Saintly Billy* (ed Ian MacCormick: 2003); *The Story of Marie Powell, Wife to Mr Milton* and *Isles of Unwisdom* (ed Simon Brittan: 2003); *Count Belisarius* and *Lawrence of Arabia* (ed Scott Ashley: 2004); *The Golden Fleece* and *Seven Days in New Crete* (ed Patrick Quinn: 2004); *The Long Weekend* and *The Reader Over Your Shoulder* (ed Michelle Ephraim: 2006); *King Jesus* and *My Head! My Head!* (ed Robert David: 2006); *Goodbye to All That and Other Great War Writings* (ed Steven Trout: 2007).

Works that Graves co-authored with Laura Riding are also published by Carcanet and include *Essays from 'Epilogue', 1935–1937* (ed Mark Jacobs: 2001); *A Survey of Modernist Poetry* and *A Pamphlet Against Anthologies* (eds C Mundye and P McGuinness: 2002).

Paul O'Prey edited with useful commentary *In Broken Images: Selected Letters of Robert Graves 1914–1946* (Hutchinson: 1982) and *Between Moon and Moon: Selected Letters of Robert Graves 1946–1972* (Hutchinson: 1984).

Literary criticism

Literary criticism includes Douglas Day, *Swifter than Reason: The Poetry and Criticism of Robert Graves* (University of

North Carolina Press: 1963). Michael Kirkham's *The Poetry of Robert Graves* (Oxford University Press: 1969) discusses the Black Goddess. Also useful are Patrick J Keane, *A Wild Civility* (Oxford University Press: 1980); Harold Bloom (ed), *Robert Graves: Modern Critical Views* (Chelsea House: 1987), and Robert Richman, 'The Poetry of Robert Graves', *The New Criterion* 7.2 (October: 1988); [www/newcriterion.com/archive/07/oct88/richman.htm].

Some specialized studies are Patrick J Quinn, *The Great War and the Missing Muse: The Early Writings of Robert Graves and Siegfried Sassoon* (Susquehanna University Press: 1994), Patrick J Quinn (ed) *New Perspectives on Robert Graves* (Susquehanna University Press: 1999), and Frank L Kersnowski, *The Early Poetry of Robert Graves: The White Goddess Beckons* (University of Texas Press: 2002).

William, Lucia and Tomás

Two of Graves' children by Beryl have written books about their youth in Deià; – William Graves, *Wild Olives: Life in Majorca with Robert Graves* (Hutchinson: 1995), and Lucia Graves, *A Woman Unknown. Voices from a Spanish Life* (Virago: 1999). Tomás Graves' *Bread and Oil: Majorcan Culture's Last Stand* (1980), has been published in many editions and countries and discusses how traditional peasant food is fashionable among the young. Tomás is also a musician as can be seen in *Tuning up at Dawn* (Fourth Estate: 2004).

Others

Raphael Patai has written about his friendship and work with Graves in *Robert Graves and the Hebrew Myths* (Wayne State University Press: 1992). The correspondence between Graves and the well-known comedian Spike Milligan is published as *Dear Robert, Dear Spike* (A Sutton: 1991).

Sir Rupert Hart-Davis has edited three volumes of *Siegfried Sassoon's Diaries, 1915–18* (Faber: 1983), *1920–22* (Faber: 1981), *1923–25* (Faber: 1985). Sassoon's relationship to Graves is studied in Jean Moorcroft Wilson, *Siegfried Sassoon: The Making of a War Poet: A Biography 1886–1918* (Routledge: 1999). Pat Barker's novel *Regeneration* (Viking: 1991) is based on Graves' friendship with Sassoon and was made into a film (1997).

A version of what happened between Graves, Riding and the Jacksons can be found in Tom Matthews' *Under the Influence: Recollections of Robert Graves, Laura Riding and Friends* (Cassell: 1979), originally published in the USA as *Jacks or Better: a Narrative* (Harper & Row: 1977); the story is also the basis of Miranda Seymour's novel *The Telling* (Picador: 1999), published in the USA as *The Summer of '39* (Norton: 1999).

Laura Riding's *Collected Poems* (1938) were republished by Carcanet (1980). Other Carcanet publications of her work include *Progress of Stories* (1935, 1982), *A Trojan Ending* (1937, 1984), *Lives of Wives* (1939, 1988), and *The Telling* (1972, 2005), the last of which contains the substance of her thoughts about truth, language and poetry. Her 'Some Autobiographical

Corrections of Literary History' can be found in *Denver Quarterly* (Winter: 1973) pp 1–33. Two major biographies are Deborah Baker's *In Extremis: The Life of Laura Riding* (Grove Press: 1993) and Elizabeth Friedmann, *A Mannered Grace: the Life of Laura (Riding) Jackson* (Persea Books: 2005). A chronology and other information can be found on the Cornell University library website. [http:www.unc.edu/~ottotwo/ LRJbiography.html?18,30]

Friends

Siegfried Sassoon, T E Lawrence and Laura Riding are famous, but many of Graves' other friends remain of interest. Norman Cameron is the subject of a book by Warren Hope, *Norman Cameron: His Life, Work and Letters* (Greenwich Exchange: 2000); Cameron's Hogarth Press *Collected Poems 1905–53* has been updated by a *Collected Poems and Selected Translations* (Anvil: 1990) edited by Warren Hope and Jonathan Barker. John Aldridge's paintings can be found in the collections of the Tate Gallery and the Victoria & Albert Museum and there is a fine portrait of Laura Riding in the National Portrait Gallery. James Reeves was a pseudonym for John Morris who wrote and edited many books of and about poetry. Alastair Reid is a prize-winning writer as well as a translator of Latin American literature. He has taught in the USA and written for the *New Yorker* and the *New York Review of Books*. There is an *Alastair Reid Reader* (Middlebury College Museum of Art: 1994). Honor Wyatt and George Ellidge are probably best known now as the parents of the progressive rock musician Robert Wyatt, a link between Deià of the 1930s and 1960s.

Matriarchy and cultural anthropology

Myth, Religion and Mother Right: Selected Writings of Johann Jakob Bachofen, translated by Ralph Manheim (Princeton University Press: 1992) is more approachable than the five volume set of *Das Mutterrecht* (1861) translated by David Partenheimer (Mellen Press: 2003–7). J G Frazer's *The Golden Bough* (1890) exists in many editions including the 12-volume (1906–15) third edition. Abridged one-volume editions were published in 1922, 1994, 1995 and 2002 (a reprint of 1922). Roger Ackerman's 'Introduction' to the Princeton University Press (1991) edition of Jane Ellen Harrison's *Prolegomena to the Study of Greek Religion* (1903) is a place to start, followed by Annabel Robinson's *The Life and Work of Jane Ellen Harrison* (Oxford University Press: 2002). Of Margaret Murray's many works her *Witch Cult in Western Europe* (Oxford University Press: 1921) appears the main influence on Graves.

Contexts

Jacqueline Waldren's *Insiders and Outsiders* discusses the inter-action of foreigners and locals in Deià (Berghahn Books: 1996). For the Georgians see Robert H Ross, *Georgian Revolt: Rise and Fall of a Poetic Ideal 1910–1922* (Southern Illinois University Press: 1965). General reading on the war poets includes

Paul Fussell's *The Great War and Modern Memory* (Oxford University Press: 1975), Adrian Caesar's *Taking It Like A Man. Suffering, Sexuality & the War Poets*, (Manchester University Press: 1993), and Samuel Hynes, *A War Imagined: The First World War and English Culture* (Bodley Head, Oxford: 1990). The broader literary and cultural history is discussed by Chris Baldick, *The Modern Movement 1910–1940* (Oxford University Press: 2004) which is Volume 10 of the *Oxford English Literary History*.

Index